Exploring Diversity
A Video Case Approach

Stephen D. Kroeger
Forest Hills Schools

Anne M. Bauer
University of Cincinnati

Upper Saddle River, New Jersey
Columbus, Ohio

Vice President and Executive Publisher: Jeffery W. Johnston
Executive Editor: Debra A. Stollenwerk
Editorial Assistant: Mary Morrill
Development Editor: Kimberly J. Lundy
Assistant Editors: Dan Parker, Amy Nelson
Production Editor: JoEllen Gohr
Design Coordinator: Diane C. Lorenzo
Cover Designer: Terry Rohrbach
Cover image: Corbis
Production Manager: Pamela D. Bennett
Director of Marketing: Ann Castel Davis
Marketing Manager: Darcy Betts Prybella
Marketing Coordinator: Tyra Poole

Pearson Prentice Hall™ is a trademark of Pearson Education, Inc
Pearson® is a registered trademark of Pearson plc
Prentice Hall® is a registered trademark of Pearson Education, Inc
Merrill® is a registered trademark of Pearson Education, Inc

Pearson Education Ltd
Pearson Education Singapore Pte. Ltd
Pearson Education Canada, Ltd
Pearson Education—Japan
Pearson Education Australia Pty. Limited
Pearson Education North Asia Ltd
Pearson Educación de Mexico, S.A. de C.V
Pearson Education Malaysia Pte. Ltd

10 9 8 7 6 5 4 3 2
ISBN: 0-13-117258-1

Exploring Diversity
A Video Case Approach

PREFACE

Introduction
This interactive CD-ROM and accompanying activity guide provides immediate access to powerful, living, classroom examples of culturally responsive teaching. The CD contains four video clips, grouped by topic (One Teacher's Influence and Majority Culture) and classroom (2nd grade literacy and 7th grade science). The activity guide provides discussion of various concepts, including culturally responsive teaching, instructional planning, classroom climate, and how to engage families; and it offers activities and questions that guide students toward understanding, analyzing, and synthesizing the video cases. The CD and guide work together as a field experience for students, where they can view quality examples of culturally responsive teaching in a classroom setting.

What Is Culturally Responsive Teaching?
Culturally responsive teaching celebrates each student as part of the learning community and recognizes the role that students' real-life experiences and cultural traditions can play in the classroom. Culturally responsive teaching recognizes that students bring with them knowledge and experiences that are essential to their construction of concepts in the classroom. It reflects the knowledge, skills, and dispositions of the INTASC (Interstate New Teacher Assessment and Support Consortium, 1992) Standards. Culturally responsive teaching recognizes that each individual's beliefs about teaching and learning have a significant impact on his or her interactions in the classroom.

Organization of the Text
This guide includes detailed instructions on how to install the CD-ROM, and how to navigate through the CD's template. It also provides contextual information and performance assessment to effectively observe and understand each video case. This contextual information will help draw meaning from these observations.

The guide is organized into three parts. Part I, Understanding Culturally Responsive Teaching, contains four chapters.

Chapter 1 responds to the question, "What is culturally responsive instruction?" In this chapter, culturally responsive instruction is defined, and each of its elements is discussed. Particular emphasis is placed on three principles of culturally responsive instruction: (a) utilizing cultural themes, (b) cooperative learning, and (c) creating a vision for celebrating diversity.

Chapter 2 describes differentiated learning as a primary strategy for putting culturally responsive instruction in action.

Chapter 3 describes aspects of classroom climate and structures for management. Cooperative learning and recognizing the role of multiple intelligences in managing classrooms are discussed. The chapter concludes with a discussion of functional behavioral assessment of specific behavioral concerns.

Chapter 4 presents research related to families from various culturally groups and issues related to cultural competence in family engagement.

Part II of this guide describes each of the video cases and gives a brief introduction for each case. This is followed by a description of the cases' key elements. Each chapter concludes with discussion questions (suggested responses presented at the end of the guide) and open-ended questions for consideration.

Part III presents the following resources: performance assessments and scoring rubrics, acknowledgements, sample responses to case questions, and a list of references.

The CD-ROM Video Cases

Four cases, each presenting a unique aspect of culturally responsive instruction, are included on the CD-ROM. These cases address primary grades, middle school, and secondary school. They also discuss cultural, ethnic, linguistic, and socioeconomic diversity.

In the first case, Janice Glaspie and Darwin Henderson are working with literate, inner city, African American children. In this classroom every child is challenged, feels safe, and experiences the joy of learning. Though well-meaning individuals may emphasize the need for direct instruction with young children in inner urban settings, they demonstrate the use of literature to enhance literacy learning. As Ms. Glaspie contends, these children are literate.

At first glance, the second video case appears to present a homogeneous classroom. The socioeconomic diversity and developmental needs of these middle school students, however, have a significant effect on the interactions in the classroom. In this science classroom, Cathy Burton works with students to make connections to other content areas, as well as worldwide issues using poster projects and presentations.

In the third case, a secondary school teacher, Ms. Joy Lohrer, saw a need for diversity in the school. Rather than impose structure, she turned to the students for ideas and suggestions. Ms. Lohrer initially provided the specific agenda of the tolerance training videos and then generated a list of student-desired activities. This educator made a commitment to meet each Thursday. Her goal was to listen to students. In this video case, Ms. Lohrer provides an example of "what one teacher can do."

In the final case, Guy Jones, Hunkpapa Lakota and a full-blood member of the Standing Rock Sioux Nation, discusses assumptions that may have an impact on the self-concept of young children. In this conversation with his colleague, Sally Moomaw, they illustrate how classroom practices—some of which are imbedded in our own experiences as students and teachers—are laid bare in view of another culture.

Features

For a better understanding of the video cases and to gain insight into the concepts and practice of culturally relevant teaching, several supports are provided in this booklet. Each section begins with the Interstate New Teacher Assessment and Support Consortium (INTASC) Standards Principles, Content, Knowledge, and Dispositions that are addressed in each video case. The guide's features also include:

- Reflection questions to help consider the material provided.
- Key points of each case, followed by questions.
- Sample responses to the discussion questions.
- List of references for further reading.
- Performance assessment activities that provide evidence for the indicated Principles of the Interstate New Teacher Assessment and Support Consortium.

Acknowledgments

This project allowed us to interact with a group of professionals committed to culturally responsive education for all children. Without their baring their souls and actions, these video cases and booklet could not have been produced. So, we gratefully acknowledge:

Cathy Burton
Janice Glaspie
Darwin Henderson
Guy W. Jones
Joy Lohrer
Sally Moomaw

CONTENTS

TO THE STUDENT

Take a moment to consider your own days as a student. Who were your classmates and teachers? Were they similar to you? Different? Was your school diverse? The school in which you work as a teacher may be very different from the one you attended as a student. You are likely to encounter many students, teachers, and staff members from different cultural, ethnic, and language groups, and you may notice a greater number of students with disabilities in general education classrooms. Schools today are increasingly diverse. At the same time, teachers are being held to higher levels of accountability for the student performance. To be a successful teacher, it is important to master the techniques of effective teaching; however, your beliefs about teaching and learning are probably the most influential factor in how you will teach. Your commitment that every student can learn—and that it is your role to make the curriculum accessible to each of them—is vital to your success and to that of your students.

What Is Culturally Responsive Teaching?

Culturally responsive teaching celebrates each student as part of the learning community and recognizes the role that their real-life experiences and cultural traditions can play in the classroom. Being culturally responsive also means providing support for those students whose educational, economic, social, political, and cultural futures are most at risk. In these ways, being a culturally responsive teacher is not much different from being an effective teacher; however, the hallmark of a culturally responsive teacher is his or her recognition that the teacher is a political being—an individual who is working toward social justice and not "just doing a job."

Even though each classroom is its own unique culture, composition, and characteristics, there are some general considerations of culturally responsive instruction. These include the central issues of justice, general considerations in place in culturally responsive classrooms. Ladson-Billings (1994) describes central considerations as:

- Helping students whose educational, economic, social, political, and cultural futures are most at risk to become intellectual leaders in the classroom.

- Supporting students as apprentices in a learning community.

- Recognizing students' real-life experiences as a legitimate part of the curriculum.

- Participating in a broad concept of literacy involving both written and oral traditions.

- Engaging collaboratively in a struggle against the status quo.

- Recognizing the teacher as a political being.

Culturally responsive instruction promotes excellent and personal meaning in education for culturally diverse students, accepting and celebrating diversity as a way of life (McLaughlin,

1996). Place is constantly considered, with students making sense of their own communities and the larger world, recognizing themselves as both products and creators of the interconnections among people and places (Raymer, 2001).

Developing Your Identity as a Culturally Responsive Professional

The classrooms and interviews presented in the video cases are meant to challenge your assumptions and help you develop a wider perspective on teaching. You may find yourself considering your own culture or ethnicity and school experience. This is an excellent opportunity to develop an attitude of reflective dialogue—considering and discussing your own ideas and experiences and the ideas and experiences of others—that will help you understand the needs and perspective of all students and peers. You may become more aware of the congruence or lack of congruence between your home and community experience and your life at school. Did you experience a teacher in your years as a student with whom you resonated? Do the teachers and individuals in these cases express similar actions and values to the teacher you remember? How do the values presented in the video cases compare with your own experiences, assumptions, and beliefs?

As you view the videos, keep in mind that these are expert teachers and mature, reflective individuals. No one begins his or her work in classrooms at this level of proficiency, and it can be difficult to determine your own role in changing school and societal assumptions about culture and diversity. These educators may be teaching their students very differently than you were taught or expressing views that may be new to you, and each has a unique insight that will help you grow as a reflective practitioner. We encourage you to maintain an open mind and to accept the challenge of becoming a culturally responsive teacher.

Welcome to Culturally Responsive Classrooms!

Interacting with children and young adults in a culturally responsive manner is a challenging and rewarding effort. Think about the voices of these educators as they communicate their absolute belief that every child can learn and should have the opportunity to shine. Enjoy seeing students actively engaged in learning. We enjoyed seeing these professionals in action, and hope you can find pieces of their work to use as you construct your own practice.

GETTING STARTED: HOW TO USE THE CD-ROM

Template Structure and Functionality
In the explanations below we will help you grasp the numerous possibilities available on this CD. In addition to this guide, you can access a tutorial on the CD by inserting the CD, opening the template and clicking on the Help (?) Button located in the lower right- hand corner of the screen.

Requirements to Run the CD-ROM
You will need to install the latest version of QuickTime if you don't have it downloaded on your computer. You will find this out when you try to play a video clip. If you don't have the appropriate version of QuickTime, an error message and sometimes a red colored "X" across the video screen will appear, indicating that you need to install QuickTime.

Installing QuickTime®
PC: At least Windows® 98 and QuickTime 6 are needed. If you are unsure of whether or not you have QuickTime 6, go ahead with the procedure to install it. Your computer will tell you if you have it or if you have a newer version. If you have QuickTime 6, quit the installation procedure. To install QuickTime in a PC, follow these steps:

Step 1. Place CD-ROM into the computer's CD-ROM player tray.
Step 2. Click on "My Computer."
Step 3. Click on the CD-ROM drive image, the program files and folders will appear.
Step 4. Click on the folder titled "PC QuickTime Installer." Click on the folder and follow the cues. QuickTime 6 will be installed on your computer. You can also install QuickTime 6 by visiting: http://www.apple.com/quicktime/download/ to download the free QuickTime 6 player.

Macintosh: At least Macintosh Operating System 9 and QuickTime 6 are needed. If you are unsure of whether or not you have QuickTime 6, go ahead with the procedure to install it. Your computer will tell you if you have it or if you have a newer version. If you already have QuickTime 6, quit the installation procedure. To install QuickTime in a Macintosh computer, follow these steps:

Step 1. Place CD-ROM into the computer's CD-ROM player tray.
Step 2. Click on the CD-ROM image that appears on the desktop. The program files and folders will appear.
Step 3. Click on the folder titled "QuickTime Installer." Click on that folder and follow the cues. QuickTime 6 will be installed on your computer. You can also install QuickTime 6 by visiting: http://www.apple.com/quicktime/download/ to download the free QuickTime 6 player.

Playing the CD-ROM Program

PC: **Step 1**. Place CD-ROM into the computer's CD-ROM player tray.

Step 2. Click on "My Computer."

Step 3. Click on the CD-ROM drive image. The program files and folders will appear.

Step 4. Click on the "Click Me!" icon (usually orange in color).

Step 5. Introductory music and credits screen will play.

MAC: **Step 1**. Place CD-ROM into the computer's CD-ROM player tray. After a few moments, the CD-ROM image will appear on the desktop.

Step 2. Click on the CD-ROM image. The program files and folders will appear.

Step 3. Click on the "Click Me!" icon (usually orange in color).

Step 4. Introductory music and credits screen will play.

NOTE: When using the CD-ROM for the first time, we recommend you start with the "Get Help" button to familiarize yourself with the template. Select the second help section entitled "Using the Interface" and quickly review the contents. When you have all the information you need to begin, click the "Orientation" button for a brief overview of the CD's content. (If you need help when viewing the CD, click on the question mark (?) button located in the lower left-hand corner of the interface to access the automated tutorials.)

For technical troubleshooting problems, contact your system administrator or contact the CD-ROM's development team by calling **1-435-654-2166,** or email **carlharris@shadowlink.net.**

Using the Opening Screen
Now you are at the title screen where you will hear introductory music. The text on the title screen includes the title of the CD, the authors and co-authors, the publisher, and the copyright. Next, click on one of three buttons – Let's Go, Get Help, or Orientation.

1. **Let's Go**—Click to begin immediately without any preliminaries.
2. **Get Help**—Click to help you understand the philosophy on how the template was created and how it works. The CD's tutorial provides a menu that allows you to access and find more information concerning the template's functionality or video ethnography history.
3. **Orientation**—Click to read a brief overview of the CD's content, organization, and functionality.

Using the Orientation Screen
You will find brief explanations on the Orientation screen about the schools, teachers, content, video, audio, and text content organization, as well as how to a obtain free copy of QuickTime 6.

Using the Help Screen
You will find that the Help button provides a menu of 35 specific topics organized within 10 categories related to the theoretical underpinnings of the template, its functions and special tools, and its intellectual history. Animation, audio, and text explanations are given to help you quickly grasp how the template works.

Layout and Organization of the Template

The template organization in the left-hand navigation bar provides random access to labeled buttons with the following functions:

- Orientation—briefly explains the content and gives a few technical cues to get started
- Array of Studies—portrays different classrooms or different variables within a given classroom (Difficult Behavior Preschool, Classroom Climate 6th Grade, Assess Plan Middle School, Support Participation High School)
- Custom Studies—activates new studies created by the user
- Study Builder—allows the user to create new studies
- Text—gives access to all the interpretation text in all the studies
- Notepad—gives the user a place to takes notes or answer questions
- Internet—provides direct access to relevant Internet sites
- Credits—provides photos and brief biographies of all contributors to the CD
- Help (?)—provides an animated tutorial of the CD's functionality and history
- Stop—allows the user to close the CD down

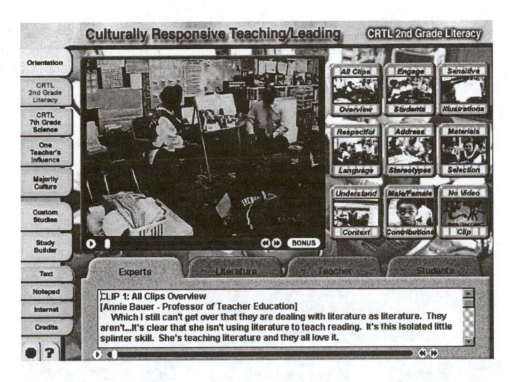

The banner at the top of the screen shows the title of the CD on the left and the title of the activated study on the right. At the top left is the video screen with its controller at its base, which gives you control over video play. On the top right are nine probe buttons. When activated, the buttons will play a video clip and activate text and audio perspectives associated with the probe.

The first probe button in the upper left is usually titled "All Clips Overview" and allows the user to play the entire video for a given study without interruption. This helps you form a holistic view of the subjects. Each of the remaining buttons focus on specific elements or variables of teaching and learning.

When a probe button is activated, the perspective fields in the lower portion of the screen activate—providing text and audio interpretations from the point of view of various stakeholders, such as experts, professional literature, teachers, and students.

Using the Probe Activation of Video & Commentaries

When a study has been activated it will change color. Selection of this study has activated the nine probes associated with it, namely: All Clips Overview, Anticipate Redirect, Natural Supports, Materials Space, Monitor Evaluate, Keystone Behaviors, Team Collaborate, Structure Routines, and Reveal Reasons (as shown in the screen capture above). When a probe button has been activated, a red frame will surround the image. Please note that the Expert tab will open as the default. Click on the audio controller at the bottom of the perspectives field to hear the subject's voice, as well as read personal comments. The scroll bar on the right side of the text field allows the user to view the remaining text.

When a video has been selected and begins to play, you can stop, start, pause, rewind, or forward the clip by clicking on the buttons below the activated video clip. Additionally, by clicking on the Bonus button, you can view extension material that is specific to a particular video clip. Here, the authors of the CD have briefly described the content of each case.

STUDY BUILDER

The Study Builder is provided so the user can go beyond exploration of the studies already created.

To create your own individual study builder, first review various video segments. To view segments:

1. Click on one of the video clips at the bottom of the Study Builder Screen.
2. Click on the Play Video button located above the clips.
3. To end the video, either click on the small X located at the upper left corner of the video screen, or click another video clip button.

Again, all video control capacities, e.g., stop, start, pause, reverse, fast forward, are available when playing video for regular studies and also for Study Builder videos.

Choosing Video Selection in the Study Builder

After previewing various clips, move the relevant clips into a new study by clicking on any video clip button and dragging it to any of the eight video button spaces in the mid-left corner of the screen. You can choose and determine the order and number of the video clips (a maximum of eight clips). To change the collection of clips assembled, drag and drop them to a different location, or click on the Reset Clips button and all clips will be returned to their original position.

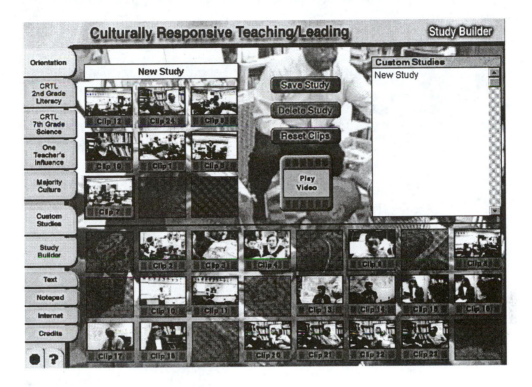

Saving a Study in the Study Builder

Once you have selected a set of video clips and placed them in the desired order, the clips can be saved. To save, click on the Save Study button and title the clip in the dialogue box that appears. The new study name will appear in the Custom Studies field in the upper right. To delete previously created studies:

1. Select the desired study.
2. Click on its title in the Custom Studies field.
3. Click on the Delete Study Button.

CUSTOM STUDIES

Once new studies have been created, they can be further elaborated and accessed by clicking on Custom Studies in the left hand navigation bar. When Custom Studies is activated, the titles of the new studies created will appear in the Custom Studies field at the bottom right side of the screen.

Activating a Study & Using Video Play in Custom Studies

To access the video clips related to a new study, click on a new study title in the Custom Studies field. Once a custom study has been selected, the video clips will appear on the video button field in the upper right corner. The set of video clips will retain their number and order originally organized.

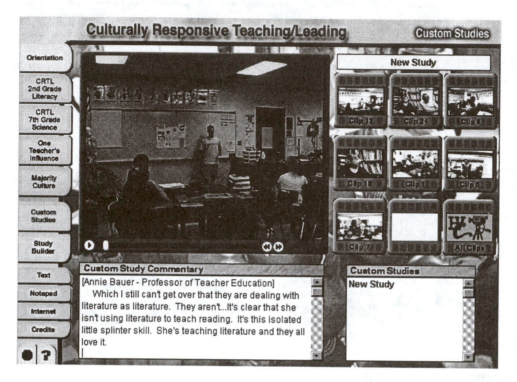

Creating Custom Study Commentary

When a specific video clip is selected, not only does the video play, but also a text field opens that gives you the opportunity to insert commentary. Here, you can explain why this particular video clip is relevant to your custom study. You can also make clarifying statements that draw attention to certain elements within the video clip. You can name the custom study and choose where you would like the file to be saved.

Using Text Archive in Custom Studies

The textual data that you use to make your custom study may consist of your own commentary, but it may also be combined with selected quotes from the perspective commentary contained in the studies.

For ease of access to all the commentaries on the CD, click on the Text button to activate a case's text archive. When one study is selected, all of the probe titles appear in the upper right hand field. Click on a given probe title to specifically access commentary text related to each probe's content. This, in turn, will display all the text associated with that probe in the text field at the bottom of the screen.

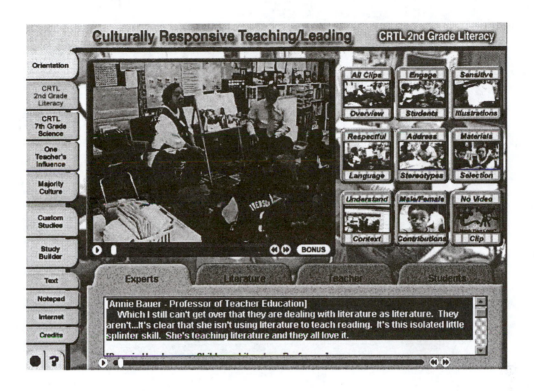

Using Select, Copy, and Paste in Text Archive in Custom Studies

You can highlight and copy any portion of the text by using the standard process used in most software. Once the text has been highlighted and copied, it can be pasted in the commentary box associated with a given video clip. You can now provide your own commentary to support your conjecture and reinforce it with selected quotes from the various commentators.

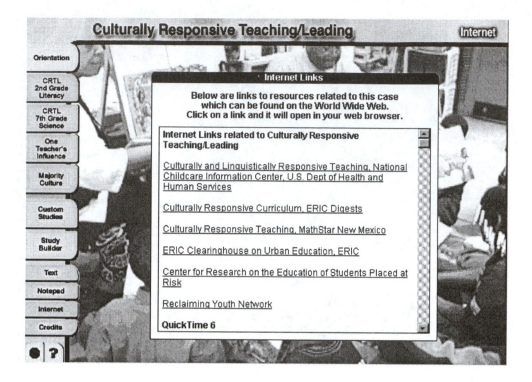

Using Internet Access

In the process of making a custom case, you do not need to be limited by using your own commentary or selected quotes from the study commentators. A ready access Internet button provides you the ability to access World Wide Web sites. Here, we have included Internet sites concerning the issues targeted in your custom study. Excerpts and quotes from Internet sites can be highlighted, copied, and pasted to the Custom Studies Commentary text field.

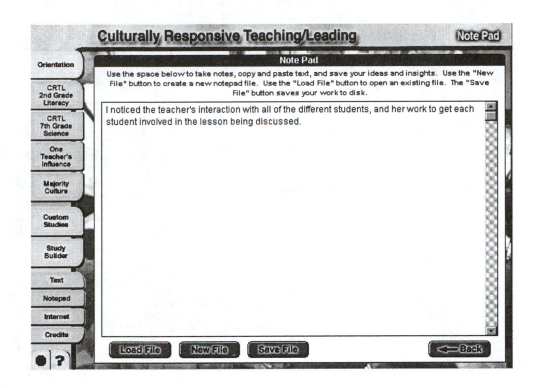

NOTEPAD

Please note that you may take notes while viewing the video cases. Click on the Notepad button in the navigation bar to activate this feature. When Notepad opens, you will need to set up a notes file by giving the file a title. Also, determine where you would like to save this information (either on a disk, hard drive, or a CD). When the work session is finished and notes have been saved, close the CD. Be sure to double-check that your work was saved in the appropriate location.

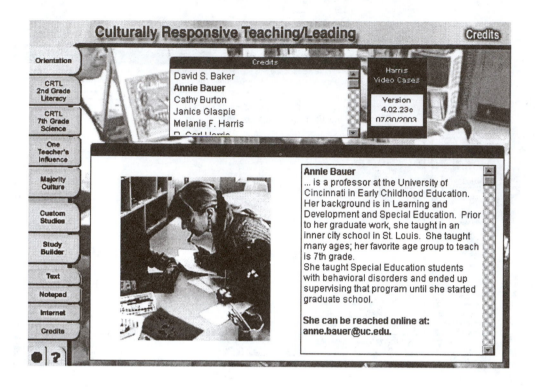

REFERENCES

All individuals making significant contributions to the production of the CD are included in the credits. Click on the Credits button to access the credits, which is located in the left-hand navigation bar. When you click on a given person's name, you can view the person's photo and biography.

PART I: UNDERSTANDING CULTURALLY RESPONSIVE TEACHING

CHAPTER 1: WHAT IS CULTURALLY RESPONSIVE TEACHING?

After completing this section, you will be able to:

- Describe issues related to schools and diversity
- Identify general considerations of culturally responsive instruction
- Describe specific principles of teaching in a culturally responsive way

INTASC PRINCIPLES, KNOWLEDGE, DISPOSITIONS, AND PERFORMANCE

Principle 3: The teacher understands how students differ in their approaches to learning and creates instructional opportunities that are adapted to diverse learners.

Knowledge:
- The teacher understands and can identify differences in approaches to learning and performance, including different learning styles, multiple intelligences, and performance modes, and can design instruction that helps use students' strengths as the basis for growth.
- The teacher understands how students' learning is influenced by individual experiences, talents, and prior learning, as well as language, culture, family, and community values.
- The teacher has a well-grounded framework for understanding cultural and community diversity and knows how to learn about and incorporate students' experiences, cultures, and community resources into instruction.

Dispositions:
- The teacher respects students as individuals with differing personal and family backgrounds and various skills, talents, and interests.
- The teacher is sensitive to community and cultural norms.
- The teacher makes students feel valued for their potential as people, and helps them learn to value each other.

Performances:
- The teacher seeks to understand students' families, cultures, and communities, and uses this information as a basis for connecting instruction to students' experiences (e.g., drawing explicit connections between subject matter and community matters, making assignments that can be related to students' experiences and cultures).
- The teacher brings multiple perspectives to the discussion of subject matter, including attention to students' personal, family, and community experiences and cultural norms.
- The teacher creates a learning community in which individual differences are respected.

SCHOOLS AND CLASSROOMS, TEACHING AND LEARNING

You are preparing to teach in a classroom that will probably not resemble the classroom you attended during your own school career. You may have attended schools in which many of the students were much like you. Not only did your classmates look like you, your teacher also probably looked like you. Many of you had two parents and lived in your own home. Most or all of you had English as your first language. The classroom has changed a great deal over the past twenty or twenty-five years. Jackson and Harper (2002) describe changes such as

- increased cultural, ethnic, and linguistic diversity.
- more students with disabilities in general education classrooms.
- greater accountability for the performance of students.

Hodgkinson (2001) argues that teachers need to be aware of educational demographics in order to better teach "other people's children." The traditional teaching force, white, middle-class women who were successful in school themselves, is often teaching "other people's children." Understanding the key educational demographics provides teachers with insights into their practice. In his frank discussion of the shifting demographics of students, Hodgkinson states that:

- if you live in a central city of the eastern half of the United states, you can expect no enrollment increases and some decreases because people who can flee to the suburbs.
- the inner suburban ring will include more students from minority cultures, more immigrants, more students learning English as a second language, and more students living in poverty. The inner suburb will begin to resemble the inner city.
- enrollments in small towns and rural areas will remain flat, with increasingly large percentages of elderly people, as older residents "age in place" and younger residents escape small-town life.
- racial and economic segregation are almost the same thing in the East and Midwest.

An additional form of diversity that affects all teachers is the transience of their students. Mobility has become far more important than births in explaining state population changes. The states with the lowest rates of high school graduation and college admissions are the five most transient states in the United States. A million people in the New England, middle Atlantic, and Midwestern states move to the southeast and southwest each year, settling mainly in California, Texas, and Florida (Hodgkinson, 2001).

These changes present a challenge to teachers, who need to develop new strategies of instruction that engage students and motivate them to learn and form communities of learners (McLaughlin, 1996). As a teacher, you are responsible for all of the students in your classroom. As the INTASC standards suggest, it is important not only to understand students' families, cultures, and communities, but also to use this knowledge to connect instruction to the child's experiences. The need to make connections is one of the primary assumptions of culturally responsive instruction.

Reflection

Consider your own experience when answering the questions below. Reflect on your first experiences with diversity.

1. What was your first experience with diversity?
2. How did you feel about that interaction?
3. Do you think students today are having similar "first experiences"? Why or why not?

Learning is a social process that involves socialization of students into "educated persons" (McLaughlin, 1996). McLaughlin (1996) suggests that participation in cultural activities with the guidance of a more skilled partner—you, the teacher—enables children to internalize tools for thinking and taking more mature approaches to problem solving that are appropriate in their culture. Problems occur, however, when children internalize the status difference between cultures. Unfortunately, this can be communicated by teachers. If their home culture and language are devalued, and teachers don't make links between the culture and school, children can lose the strength and coherence of a bicultural identity.

Your beliefs about teaching and learning are probably the most influential factor in how you will teach (Lipson & Wixon, 1997). These beliefs will shape the learning context you develop and maintain in your classroom (Schmidt, Rozendal, & Greenman, 2002). As the INTASC standards suggest, it is your job to communicate to your students not only that you value them as people, but also to help them to learn to value each other.

GENERAL CONSIDERATIONS OF CULTURALLY RESPONSIVE INSTRUCTION

As we discuss culturally responsive education, two terms recur: *culture* and *ethnicity*. *Culture* refers to the ways in which we perceive, believe, evaluate, and behave (Goodenough, 1987). Culture provides us with generally accepted and patterned ways of acting that enable us to live together and provides the norms that guide our language, actions, feelings, and thinking. *Ethnicity,* on the other hand, is more subjective. According to Heath and McLaughlin (1993), ethnicity is a subjective view a group holds regarding its common membership because of shared descent or historical background and similarities of customs, language, and, sometimes, physical type. The members of the group may not acknowledge the features that seem to set them apart, and certain groups may label other groups as "ethnic groups."

Understanding culture is a challenge. Geertz (1973) argues that only a native can make first order interpretations of his or her own culture. He refers to our being suspended in webs of significance. Each of us must ask, "What is the message?" communicated by a student's behavior. Well-meaning teachers may trod on the culture of one of their students without meaning to by, for example, asking an Asian child to give eye contact during a discussion, having a Native American child cut out construction paper feathers, or assuming a Muslim does not shake hands.

Each classroom has its own unique culture, composition, and characteristics, but there are some general principals of culturally responsive instruction. These include the central issue of justice and the general considerations described by Ladson-Billings (1994):

- helping students whose educational, economic, social, political, and cultural futures are most at risk to become intellectual leaders in the classroom.

- supporting students as apprentices in a learning community.

- recognizing students' real-life experiences as a legitimate part of the curriculum.

- participating in a broad concept of literacy involving both written and oral traditions.

- engaging collaboratively in a struggle against the status quo.

- recognizing the teacher as a political being.

Culturally responsive instruction promotes excellence and personal meaning in education for culturally diverse students, accepting and celebrating diversity as a way of life (McLaughlin, 1996). *Place* is constantly considered, with students making sense of their own communities and the larger world, recognizing themselves as both products and creators of the interconnections among people and places (Raymer, 2001).

Gay (2000) further describes culturally responsive teaching as instruction that uses the cultural knowledge, experiences, and learning styles of students to make learning more appropriate and effective for them. According to Gay, culturally responsive teaching:

- acknowledges the legitimacy of cultural heritages as legacies that affect students' dispositions, attitudes, and approaches to learning and as worthy content to be taught in the formal curriculum.

- builds on meaningfulness between home and school experiences as well as between academic abstractions and lived sociocultural realities.

- uses a variety of instructional strategies that are connected to different learning styles.

- teaches students to know and praise their own and each others' cultural heritages.

- incorporates multicultural information, resources, and materials in all the subjects and skills taught in school.

Culturally responsive teachers promote a learning community, honor human dignity, and promote individual self-concepts.

SPECIFIC PRINCIPLES

There are several specific principles that support the learning of students from various ethnic, cultural, and linguistic groups. These include:

- utilizing cultural themes in instruction.

- utilizing cooperative learning.

- recognizing a school-wide vision of quality schooling for all students.

Utilizing Cultural Themes in Instruction

Cultural themes can be used to make instruction more relevant to students in both structure and content. Students' cultural socialization poses a challenge when the school operates in one cultural mode to the exclusion of others, or when students from other cultures are expected to set aside their cultural habits in order to succeed in school (Gay, 1994). Gay identifies several "incompatibilities" that most often affect teaching and learning as (a) values orientations; (b) interpersonal relations; (c) communication styles; (d) time usage; (e) performance styles; (f) procedural rules; and (g) systems of problem solving and cognitive processing. The student's education experiences must both reflect and connect with his or her life experiences and perspectives.

Boykin and Bailey (2000) addressed this issue for African American students, identifying three Afro-cultural themes in the lives of their students. These themes included:

- communalism, the importance placed on social bonds and interconnections with others, or the acculturation toward social relations rather than objects. In communalism, identity is tied to the social group rather than individual rights and privileges.

- movement, with an emphasis on rhythmic speech, movement, patter, and music. Students and family members demonstrated a rich movement and gestural repertoire in their interactions.

- verve, an intensity or liveliness, with an interest in a variety of intense experiences.

Students reported that they preferred communal learning contexts that promoted sharing of knowledge and materials as well as working and studying together in groups so that all members achieved. The students preferred school contexts that allowed for expressiveness in music and movement. They endorsed learning contexts that used high-energy pedagogical and learning strategies.

Using cultural themes, however, may be a challenge. Ellison and associates (2000) reported that the mainstream cultural themes of individualism, competition, and bureaucracy are most prevalent in classrooms. When other cultural themes are present, students usually initiate them. The teacher's emphasis on time and time management, as well as what Ellison refers to as the "cult of quietness," may be in direct contrast to students' cultural ways of interacting.

Cooperative Learning

McLaughlin (1996) suggests that working in cooperative groups is a key way to support students in coming to complex understandings of the material presented. Cooperative learning mirrors and reinforces the social constructivist process by which children learn. In their study of learning contexts, Boykin and Bailey (2000) reported that students preferred communal contexts that promoted sharing knowledge and materials as well as working and studying together. Abda-Haqq (1994) contends that cooperative learning is a key aspect of culturally responsive teaching.

A Vision for Celebrating Diversity

A vision conveys an intuitive, appealing picture of what an organization can become (Yukl, 1994). A student-focused mission, one that celebrates each individual's contribution to the community, may increase teacher efficacy and pride in the learning and achievement of their students (Peterson, 1986). The way in which this vision is implemented reflects the beliefs, attitudes, and values of each teacher. An effective vision is "right for the times, right for the organization, and right for the people who are working in it" (Bennis & Nanus, 1985, p. 107).

One of the key aspects of this vision is high expectations for everyone. Delpit (1991) contends that teachers may have the best intentions of attempting to meet students' needs, but actually accept products that are not adequate. Using the example of writing, she describes how teachers fail to push students who are just becoming fluent writers to the point of fully editing their work.

LEARNING ABOUT CULTURALLY RESPONSIVE INSTRUCTION

In these video cases, you will see classrooms and listen to professionals who have a commitment to the education of each student. You will be seeing and hearing that:

- culturally responsive instruction is good instruction for every child; all children are valued, and their contributions to the classroom community are recognized.

- teachers have a commitment to meeting the needs of each child, care deeply about each child, and reflect on their instructional and managerial decisions about each student.

- individualization is an ongoing teaching process.

- it is important to begin with common ground, and then move to celebrate the unique contributions of each student.

- each of us is grounded in our culture, and, if we recognize the contributions each of us makes in the community of learners, then there is no "dominant" culture.

27

View these video cases as a learner. Some of the information may challenge your assumptions and beliefs. We invite you to reflect and consider those assumptions and beliefs as you work through this guide and the video cases.

CHAPTER 2: CONSIDERATIONS IN INSTRUCTIONAL PLANNING

After completing this section, you will be able to:
- Imagine a multicultural classroom using metaphor
- Begin to construct a framework to construct a multicultural classroom
- Access an understanding of the differentiated classroom

INTASC PRINCIPLES, KNOWLEDGE, DISPOSITIONS, AND PERFORMANCE

Principle 4: The teacher understands and uses a variety of instructional strategies to encourage students' development of critical thinking, problem solving, and performance skills.

Dispositions:
- The teacher values flexibility and reciprocity in the teaching process as necessary for adapting instruction to student responses, ideas, and needs.

Performances:
- The teacher uses multiple teaching and learning strategies to engage students in active learning opportunities that promote the development of critical thinking, problem solving, and performance capabilities and that help students assume responsibility for identifying and using learning resources.

IMAGINE A MULTICULTURAL CLASSROOM

Traditional classrooms in the United States have developed from Western European traditions. The classroom culture you are most likely to see and experience is based on white, Anglo-Saxon, protestant roots with core values of individualism and freedom. There is an assumption that anyone from outside the majority culture will somehow conform to or assimilate these values and ways of perceiving the world.

Assimilation is the process by which groups adopt or adjust to the majority culture. Schools have traditionally served to transmit the values of the majority culture to students regardless of the student's cultural heritage (Gollnick, 2002). Assimilation refers to the process of having students from diverse ethnic and cultural groups merge into a majority cultural group and essentially leave their own culture behind (Mastropieri, 2000).

Spradley and McCurdy (2000) define culture as the system of learned beliefs and customs that characterize the total way of life for a particular society. Culture is the acquired knowledge that people use to interpret their world and generate social behavior. Culture is not behavior itself, but the knowledge used to construct and understand behavior. Culture is thus the system of knowledge by which people design their own actions and interpret the behavior of others.

Cultural values are conceptions of what is desirable in human experience. Conformity and assimilation in a culture result from the internalization of the majority values. Individuals frequently feel threatened when confronted with others who live according to different conceptions of desirable behavior. Humans tend to be ethnocentric. In other words, we believe that the way we do things is the natural way for all humans to do things. Those who behave differently, we reason, are simply wrong.

Spradley and McCurdy (2000) describe four interrelated propositions when considering cultural differences:

- each person's value system is a result of his or her experience and learning.

- the values that individuals learn differ from one society to another because of different experiences.

- values, therefore, are relative to the society in which they occur.

- therefore, respect the values of each of the world's cultures.

Shared values give each person a sense of belonging, a sense of being a member of a particular community. Children, for example, are not taught a wide range of possible behaviors, rather they are taught to conform to a very limited number of behavior options. These context-specific behavior patterns and values are found in all cultures. Individuals become specialists, in the sense that they are committed to a few values, and acquire the knowledge and skills of a single society (Spradley & McCurdy, 2000).

This specialization has led to the vast diversity we see throughout the world. In light of this specialization process, it is difficult to underestimate the challenge of moving from one cultural world to another. The human environment we live in is continually being altered. These changes, many of which occur rapidly, require new social and cultural skills. When we consider how long it takes cultural values to be established in a society, it is no wonder that successful adaptation to this diversity and change is a significant challenge. Those who make those adaptations are considered to be *culturally competent*.

What is required to successfully adapt to diversity? Spradley and McCurdy (2000) suggest that:

- instead of stressing assimilation into the mainstream of American life, we must recognize the extent to which our culture is pluralistic.

- we must continually examine the consequences of each value system. For example, we must continually examine values such as human growth, male superiority, homes, standard English, and how aspects of assimilation can hurt people.

- convince people to relinquish those values that have destructive consequences. A society with so much diversity will need to create a morality that can articulate conflicting values systems and create a climate of tolerance, respect, and cooperation—only then can we adapt in today's world.

Reflection

Consider your own experience when answering the questions below. Take Spradley and McCurdy's (2000) four interrelated propositions about cultural values into account in your responses.

1. What values do you hold dear? Can you describe an experience where these values were in conflict with another person's value system? Were you able to resolve this difference?
2. Are you willing to change the value system that developed from the cultural forces in which you were raised? What would you describe as the main facilitators and barriers for such a change in views?
3. Can you think of an activity that would allow students in your classroom to explore their own value systems?

RESPONDING TO CULTURAL DIVERSITY

According to the National Association for the Education of Young Children, children at younger and younger ages are negotiating difficult transitions between their home and educational settings, requiring adaptation to two or more diverse sets of rules, values, expectations, and behaviors. In the past, the expectation of cultural assimilation and the negative attitudes expressed toward certain languages led children to abandon their native language. This choice often led to feelings of loneliness, fear, and abandonment. Furthermore, the child often lost his or her home language as well.

The National Association for the Education of Young Children believes that, for the optimal development and learning of all children, educators must accept the legitimacy of children's home languages, respect and value the home cultures, and promote and encourage the active involvement and support of all families, including extended and nontraditional family units. The National Association for the Education of Young Children makes several recommendations *(Responding to linguistic and cultural diversity: Recommendations for effective early childhood education*, 1995) regarding respect for the value of home languages.

- Recommendations for working with children:

  o recognize that all children are cognitively, linguistically, and emotionally connected to the language and culture of their homes.
  o acknowledge that children can demonstrate their knowledge and capabilities in many ways.
  o understand that without comprehensible input, second-language learning can be difficult.

- Recommendations for working with families:

  o actively involve parents and families in the early learning program and setting.
  o encourage and assist all parents in becoming knowledgeable about the cognitive value for children of knowing more than one language, and provide them with strategies to support, maintain, and preserve home-language learning.
  o recognize that parents and families must rely on caregivers and educators to honor and support their children in the cultural values and norms of the home.

- Recommendations for professional preparation:

  o provide early childhood educators with professional preparation and development in the areas of culture, language, and diversity.
  o recruit and support early childhood educators who are trained in languages other than English.

- Recommendations for programs and practice:

  o recognize that children can and will acquire the use of English even when their home language is used and respected.
  o support and preserve home language usage.
  o develop and provide alternative and creative strategies for young children's learning.

Culturally responsive classrooms that achieve high quality care and education for all children, such as the National Association for the Education of Young Children has outlined, will require the collaboration of educators and families *(Responding to linguistic and cultural diversity: Recommendations for effective early childhood education*, 1995).

UNDERSTANDING DIVERSITY

According to McLaughlin and McLeod (1996), if students were distributed evenly across the nation's classrooms, every class of 30 students would include about 10 students from ethnic or racial minority groups. Of these 10, about 6 would be from language minority families; 2 to 4 of these students would have limited English proficiency, of whom two would be from immigrant families. Of the six language minority students in the class, four would speak Spanish as their native language, and one would speak an Asian language. The other language minority student would speak any one of more than a hundred languages (McLaughlin & McLeod, 1996).

McLaughlin and McLeod (1996) go on to explain that of the 30 students in this classroom, 10 (including nearly all of the language minority students) would be poor. Being poor, they would face a multiplicity of challenges such as inadequate health care and social and cultural services; strained employment opportunities; and high crime rates in their neighborhoods. In spite of these discouraging statistics, McLaughlin and McLeod (1996) find reason for optimism because many schools are seeking ways to educate all of their students. Educators are discovering new ways to teach and are including the family in the learning process.

Using a sociocultural perspective, McLaughlin and McLeod (1996) focus on the kind of "apprenticeship" learning that children naturally do as they mature into adult roles. Children are aided in this process by having the guidance of a "master," someone who is more skilled and who can assist the child in doing a particular task until he or she can do it independently. The authors suggest that for high school science students, a master may be a teacher who helps students stretch their capabilities or a professional scientist working with student interns. For a first grader learning to read, a master may be a second grader who can remember how he or she unlocked the code.

School success for children from culturally and linguistically diverse backgrounds should be viewed as a socially negotiated process involving interactions with persons, environments, resources, and goals. When they enter school, children have to adjust to the school context the behaviors and understandings that are unique to their culture. There are differences among cultures in the ways in which parents teach children at home, the ways in which parents expect children to behave, and the ways in which children and adults converse and interact. When teachers do not share their students' cultural background, the teaching-learning process may be impeded by misunderstanding and frustration (McLaughlin & McLeod, 1996).

McLaughlin and McLeod (1996, p. 4) describe an investigation by Scarcella and Chin about how Korean immigrant parents help their children with schoolwork at home. They found that Korean parents tended to give corrective feedback as soon as the child made a mistake. For example, a parent might say, "This one's wrong. You missed this one here," and then tell the child how to do it right. In contrast, parents from European American backgrounds who were not recent immigrants tended to withhold comment until the child finished, as in "Good. You missed three out of twenty. See, these three are wrong," and to encourage children to correct mistakes by themselves: "Okay, you made a mistake. See if you can figure out what you did wrong" (McLaughlin & McLeod, 1996).

This investigation of Korean and English cultural differences illustrates how diverse cultural systems can become a source of stress. Children tend to internalize these cultural conflicts. This difference, once understood, can be a source of pride and strength rather than being seen as a disability or weakness.

Another study illustrated by McLaughlin and McLeod (1996, p. 5) explains how Luis Moll, Norma Gonzalez, and their colleagues have assisted Arizona teachers in making the connection between home and school. Teachers visit students' homes as if they were anthropologists, gaining an understanding of their Latino students' cultural backgrounds as well as gathering material for their curriculum. One teacher drew on the expertise of parents employed in construction occupations to create a mathematics curriculum based on building a house. Another found that many of her students' families had extensive knowledge of the medicinal value of plants and herbs, and taught scientific concepts in that context. Still another based a curriculum unit on the discovery that some students regularly returned from Mexico with candy to sell. Students investigated the economics of marketing, compared Mexican and American candy, did a nutritional analysis of candy, studied the process of sugar processing, and conducted a survey on favorite candies, for which they graphed data and wrote a report (McLaughlin & McLeod, 1996).

These educators are allowing the diversity of cultures present in their classrooms to create a web of learning that extends across barriers and fears. Educators are called on to build on rather than replace student native languages. Students learn language best when they use it to communicate and function in the environment. Isolated instruction does little good. Problem solving and student centered investigations create high interest and motivate students to use language to express new ideas and concepts.

THE CONTACT ZONE METAPHOR

Is there a metaphor we can use to help conceptualize this culturally responsive classroom? Is there an image of the classroom where students of diverse backgrounds and languages are able to build community in a place were cultures meet and learn from one another? Pratt (1998) offers the metaphor of the contact zone. Contact zones occupy the social spaces where cultures meet and grapple with each other to be heard. The contact zone is often a place where cultures meet in contexts of highly asymmetrical relations of power. Historical asymmetrical power relations, such as colonialism and slavery, continue to be felt as their aftermaths are lived out in many parts of the world today (Pratt, 1998).

A contact zone cannot be forced. In fact, Williams (1997) cautions against attempts to "enlighten" students from the majority culture about their "problem" beliefs concerning race, gender and class. This approach has significant weaknesses. First, the attempt to convert someone to operate in a different framework only reinforces the perspective of the majority culture as central and normal, and tends to make "multicultural" synonymous with "minority" or "other." Second, this conversion model does not ask students from the majority culture to explore their own cultural influences. Instead, the approach emphasizes ideological transformation. Rather than actual change, two potentially polarizing responses result: confession or resistance, neither of which is an authentic learning goal.

In this context, Bizzell (1994) finds distinct advantages to using the contact zone as a metaphor for the classroom. First, in the contact zone, we are all products of distinctive cultural forces. The emphasis in the contact zone is on cultural forces, not moral worth. Second, different groups within the contact zone contend for the power to interpret what is going on. The question about who speaks and who is listened to is grappled with. Third, in the contact zone, awareness of what is at stake for each speaker increases potential for true negotiations. There is a clearer sense of what each group wants, resulting in less conflict and more cooperation (Bizzell, 1994).

While designing a contact zone curriculum for her English class, Bizzell (1994) realized that the questions that were asked were as important as the answers given. Instead of asking, for example, how to fit a text by Frederick Douglass into her American Renaissance course, she asked, "How should I reconceive my study of literature and composition now that I regard Douglass as an important writer?" Bizzell's efforts to construct a multicultural classroom organizes English studies in terms of historically defined contact zones, moments when different groups within society contend for the power to interpret what is going on. The goal is not to get a true representation of each group, but to see how each group represents itself imaginatively in relationship to others.

The contact zone offers an alternative to assimilation. In a contact zone, Flores (1996) points out that there is an assumption that other voices already exist. There is no argument, for example, about whether or not another's voice should be heard in the curriculum. Even if such voices were ignored or silenced in the past, they exist in the contact zone.

Seeing the classroom as a contact zone shifts the multicultural classroom experience from the tokenism so often seen in food, dance, and culture parties to dialogue and negotiation about how to honor and learn about the many cultures that are present in our schools (Flores, 1996). Raymer's (2001) conceptualization of the pedagogy of place is a helpful example of one way to honor and learn about local culture, as well as the culture that surrounds you in the classroom.

PEDAGOGY OF PLACE

Raymer (2001) discusses the pedagogy of place and the importance of promoting place-based education. There is a growing recognition of context and locale and the unique contributions these make to the educational process. The pedagogy of place approach asserts that learning occurs when students connect subject matter to their own lives and surroundings and critically reflect upon both the connection and the new materials being studied. Through this education, grounded in context, students' experiences, and community, learners come to understand themselves as inheritors, inquirers, and contributors to knowledge in overlapping webs of social, cultural, natural, scientific, and technical understanding. Using what is local and immediate as a source of curriculum tends to deepen knowledge through the larger understandings of the familiar and accessible. This in turn encourages constructive interaction with materials and resource persons beyond those found in the school (Raymer, 2001).

When individuals come to an understanding of themselves as both products and creators of interconnections among people and places, they begin to make sense of their own communities and the larger world. Individuals are then equipped to acknowledge other views shaped by histories different from their own. The process facilitates the creation of shared meaning and awareness of multiple meanings. Neither experience nor information alone create knowledge; pedagogy of place seeks to weave critical reflection, active engagement, and real world application into the learning process and the educational environment (Raymer, 2001).

One activity Raymer (2001) recommends is a community mapping exercise called the *Scout About*. Participants carry out an informal community survey to get to know their community and to find out what issues people feel strongly about. They go for a walk in the community with the goal of noticing as much as possible and listening to conversations without taking notes or asking questions. They are looking for information about their community's workplaces, recreation, religion and church, relationships, education, values, strengths, and needs. Participants also read local newspapers, especially letters to the editor and community news, and develop a list of what people are worried, happy, upset, or hopeful about. Then, they draw a map of the community, showing the locations of institutions and types of activities in addition to physical structures and landscape elements (Raymer, 2001).

Other learning modules that Raymer (2001) discusses include:

- Who are we?—an exercise that asks participants to name a place of significance.

- Where are we?—an exercise that builds sensitivity to location. Someone from the locale is asked to describe the building, the neighborhood, the community, the area, the watershed, and the bioregion.

- Using Personal Histories—place-based education draws upon the experiences of the learners, and it is through the histories of the participants that a teaching stance is developed.

The image of a culturally responsive learning environment and the methods we use to understand this reality are based in an understanding of principles and specific expressions of those principles. Bennett (2001) offers a conceptual framework for consideration as we go about our work in the service of learning.

A FRAMEWORK TO CONSTRUCT A MULTICULTURAL CLASSROOM

Multicultural education was a hopeful and idealistic response to the Civil Rights Movement of the 1950s and 1960s. The Civil Rights Movement spread to include many other minority groups, including women. The *Brown* decision in 1954 reversed the legality of "separate but equal" schools and led to rising expectations for equal opportunity and social justice (Bennett, 2001). Since then, educators all over the United States have been working to create learning environments that honor and respect the cultures of those present in their classrooms.

According to Bennett (2001), a new framework for the multicultural classroom rests on four broad principles of multicultural education. The first foundational principle is the theory of cultural pluralism. Cultural pluralism affirms the right of every ethnic group to retain its own heritage. The second foundational principle is the idea of social justice and the need to end racism, sexism, and other forms of prejudice and discrimination that were built to maintain white male privilege. Social justice focuses on the deep-seated structural injustices and systematic patterns of dominance and suppression that deny people of color material and political equality. The third foundational principle is that of affirmations of culture in the teaching and leaning process. The fourth foundational principle is visions of educational equity and excellence leading to high levels of academic learning for all children and youth. This refers to the equal opportunities of every student to reach his or her fullest potential. These principles form the basic premises that constitute the conceptual framework for a multicultural learning environment (Bennett, 2001).

For example, when considering school and classroom climates, positive climate refers to school and classroom structures and practices, as well as the attitudes, values, and beliefs of teachers and administrators. Appropriate structures, attitudes, and values contribute to high and equitable levels of student achievement and positive inter-group relations. These relationships are based on caring, respect, and trust. Each of these qualities facilitates learning. (See the table on page 42 for a summary of the conceptual framework that Bennett presents.)

Creating a positive school environment requires:

• opportunities to become acquainted and develop friendships.

• equal status among students from the different groups.

• authority figures who encourage, model, and support comfortable inter-group contact and relationships.

To illustrate school climate, a study of Latino immigrant youth by Susan Katz (1999) examined how teachers' attitudes and practices that Latino students perceived as racist were linked to structural conditions within the school that went beyond the responsibility of the individual teachers.

Coolidge Middle School, rated as one of the best in the city, was located in a quiet middle-class Asian and European-American neighborhood. Because of a federal court decision to desegregate in 1984, 270 of the school's 1,400 students were bused in from the barrio of Las Palmas or from Oakdale, an African American community. Las Palmas was a vibrant community, but also high in crime.

Through tracking and ability grouping, segregation was maintained in this desegregated school. Of the approximately 500 students enrolled in the gifted program, 43 percent was Asian and 49 percent was European American. Two percent was African American and one percent was Latino (5 percent was "other").

Among the Latino students, 31 percent were in ESL classes located in dingy cottages outside the school building and another 6.5 percent were in special education classes that were located in the school basement. Twenty-one percent of the African American students were in special education. Latino and African American students rarely participated in school activities and none were in school government. Seventy-five percent of those on the dean's discipline list were Latino or African American. Of the four females and four males Katz studied, who each had excellent records in elementary school, three dropped out in the eighth grade and only two made it to senior year (Katz, 1999).

A multicultural classroom needs to be sensitive to cultural styles in teaching and learning, as is illustrated by the work of Wade Boykin and his associates (1994) at Howard University. Boykin developed a conceptual framework for the study of African-American child socialization. The study reflects the bicultural nature of the African-American community and captures the uniformity, diversity, complexity, and richness of Black family life. This framework is based on the premise that an African-American culture encompasses three different realms of experience: mainstream, minority, and Black cultural or Afro cultural (Boykin, 1994; 1988).

Linking West African cultural ethos and core characteristics of African-American culture, Boykin (1994, 1988) identified nine interrelated but distinct dimensions manifest in terms of stylistic behaviors in the lives of African Americans. They include:

- spirituality—a vitalistic rather than mechanistic approach to life.

- harmony—the belief that humans and nature are harmoniously conjoined.

- movement expressiveness—an emphasis on the interweaving of movement, rhythm, percussiveness, music, and dance.

- verve—the special receptiveness to relatively high levels of sensate stimulation.

- affect—an emphasis on emotion and feelings.

- communication—a commitment to social connectedness where social bonds transcend individual privileges.

- expressive individualism—the cultivation of distinctive personality and a proclivity for spontaneity in behavior.

- orality—a preference for oral/aural modalities of communication.

- social time perspective—an orientation in which time is treated as passing through a social space rather than a material one.

Sensitivity to cultural learning preferences and styles such as these can support effective teaching and classroom design.

Cross, Strauss, and Fhagen-Smith (1999) discuss the racial identity of African Americans across the life span. They developed an original typology of Black racial identity. While Cross and associates focused on Nigrescence (the process of becoming Black), their description of this process may be applicable to the developmental process of other groups as well.

The authors identified five developmental stages of racial identity. The first stage is referred to as *Pre-encounter*. At this stage, the individual accepts the Anglo-European worldview and seeks assimilation into white mainstream society. According to Cross et al. (1999), white mainstream society is anti-Black and Anti-African.

The second stage is referred to as *Encounter*. The Encounter stage is triggered by a shattering experience that destroys the person's previous ethnic self-image and changes the interpretation of the condition of African Americans in the United States.

The third stage is called *Immersion-Emersion*. Individuals in this stage want to live totally in the Black world. The authors call this a pseudo-Black identity because it is based in hatred and negation of Whites rather than an affirmation of a pro-Black perspective. At this stage, individuals engage in Blacker-Than-Thou antics and view Blacks who accept Whites as Uncle Toms.

The fourth stage is *Internalization*. Here the individual internalizes his or her ethnic identity and achieves greater inner security and self-satisfaction. There is a healthy sense of Black pride and less hostility toward whites.

Internalization and Commitment is the final stage of racial identity development. The individual in this stage differs from those in stage four by becoming actively involved in plans to bring about social changes (Cross et al., 1999).

Classroom and school climates are critical to student learning and to developing the student's identity. Tatum (1992) identified four strategies for reducing student resistance and promoting student development. First, a safe classroom environment must be created (facilitated by small class size, clear guidelines for discussion). Second, create opportunities for self-generated knowledge. In one learning experience, white students go apartment hunting with Black students to experience discrimination firsthand. Third, provide an appropriate model that helps students understand their own process of ethnic identity development (guilt, shame, embarrassment, and anger are all normal). Fourth, explore strategies of empowerment. Raised awareness without knowledge of how to change can lead to despair. The reading of news and biographies and autobiographies of models of change can be helpful.

Efforts to improve our schools will evolve as we work as part of a group to improve instruction for the entire school, not just a single set of students. Miramontes (1997) contends that attempts to improve schools that serve linguistically diverse students are bound to fail unless an understanding and utilization of essential program elements is incorporated into school planning. Education for students who are linguistically diverse becomes a shared, school-wide responsibility. Educators must understand how to include all students, weigh program choices, and anticipate and evaluate the consequences. Miramontes (1997) suggests a number of guidelines to consider when designing a linguistically diverse learning environment:

- learning is a process of development that is both dynamic and constructive.

- the primary language, developed in the context of social interaction, is fundamental to the thinking, learning, and identity of every individual.

- students' first and second languages interact with one another; the instructional opportunities students receive in each language will play a critical role in determining their levels of bilingualism and academic achievement.

- individuals need to function in a multicultural society; students' knowledge of their own culture as well as the cultures of others is important not only to their school performance but to their overall success.

- the sociopolitical context has a direct impact on pedagogical decisions about education; educators' underlying attitudes toward students' families, cultures, and languages shape their instructional approaches and can result in very different academic outcomes for students from differing backgrounds (Miramontes, 1997).

Designing a culturally responsive classroom and school is a labor that requires coordinated efforts and commitment to inclusion and diversity. An understanding of differentiated learning, how a teacher uses various ways to explore the curriculum content, is another helpful way to approach diversity.

Reflection

Consider your own experience when answering the questions below. Frame your response in terms of Cross, Strauss and Fhagen-Smith's (1999) discussion of the development of racial identity across the life span.

1. Describe your own development as a person in terms of racial or cultural values and behaviors.
2. Describe an experience where you had a newfound understanding of another's culture. What caused this new understanding to occur?

The conceptual framework of research genres (Bennett, 2001)

	Cluster One: **Curriculum Reform**		Cluster Three: **Social Equity**	
Curriculum Theory	Focus on subject matter inquiry aimed at rethinking and transforming the traditional curriculum that is primarily Anglo-Eurocentric in scope. Two assumptions: (1) knowledge is contested and constructed; (2) One form of curriculum in a multicultural society is a tool of hegemony		In contrast to the other three genres, which focus on curriculum, pedagogy and the individual, this genre focuses on society. The focus here is on access, participation, and achievement in social institutions. Social action and reform are the tools this genre uses to create societal conditions of freedom, equality and justice for all, in a word: empowerment!	Social action
Detecting bias in texts, media and educational materials				Demographics
Historical inquiry in content areas		*** _**Genres**_ of research in multicultural education		Culture and race in popular culture
School and classroom climates	Cluster Two: **Equity Pedagogy** Addresses the disproportionately high rates of school dropouts, suspensions and expulsions among students of color and students from low-income backgrounds. There is an aim to achieve fair and equal educational opportunities for all of our nation's youth	**Supporting Principles:** cultural pluralism	Cluster Four: **Multicultural Competence** Like thinking skills and decision-making, this genre may become a basic skill that schools are required to teach. They may require multiple ways of perceiving, evaluating, and doing. There is an emphasis on the nature of development	Ethnic group culture
Student achievement		social justice affirmations of culture		Prejudice reduction
Cultural styles in teaching and learning		educational equity		Ethnic identity development

Graphic by S. Kroeger based on Bennett (2001)

DIFFERENTIATED INSTRUCTION

Differentiated instruction recognizes that students vary in their background knowledge, readiness, language, preferences, interacts, and responses to instruction. In a differentiated classroom, teachers use various ways to explore the curriculum content. Teachers and students engage in sense-making activities through which students can construct knowledge and students have a range of options through which to demonstrate what they have learned (Tomlinson, 1995). Tomlinson (1995) suggests that four characteristics shape teaching and learning in differentiated classrooms:

1. *Instruction is focused on concepts and driven by principles.* The goal is not to "cover" material, but the make sure that each student has the opportunity to explore and apply the key concepts of the subject.

2. *Assessment of student readiness and growth are built into the curriculum.* Assessment is constant, with the teacher providing support when the student needs additional help and offering exploration when the student is ready to move ahead.

3. *Students work in a variety of patterns.* Sometimes students work independently, sometimes in pairs, sometimes in groups.

4. *Students actively explore the content, and teachers guide that exploration.* The teacher is a facilitator of the varied activities that occur simultaneously. The student-centeredness increases students' ownership of their own learning and supports their developing independence.

There are three elements of the curriculum that teachers can differentiate. Tomlinson (2001) describes several guidelines for differentiating each of these elements:

Content: Differentiation requires that several elements and materials be used to support instructional content. These tasks must be aligned to learning goals. The instruction is concept-focused, and teachers must focus on the concepts, principles, and skills students need. For example, in the high school physics classroom, students are using outside resources, computers, and adapted materials. In the sixth grade classroom, students are provided the opportunity to practice using a sledge in addition to having a verbal explanation.

Process: Flexible grouping is consistently used. In addition, classroom management benefits both students and teachers. Students may work in teams, independently, or in pairs. Grouping varies with the activity. Students may also be given a choice in how they will approach a task.

Products: Ongoing formal and informal assessments provide the teacher with information about students' readiness and growth. Students function as active and responsible explorers, with each child feeling challenged most of the time. Expectations and requirements vary for each student's responses. Students may self-select their products, or may be provided support in completing the activity they have chosen.

In addition to these three general curricular elements, Tomlinson provides several guidelines for practice. First, the teacher should clarify key concepts and generalizations to ensure that all students are learning. Assessment becomes a teaching tool to extend rather than to measure learning. Critical and creative thinking is a goal in lesson design, requiring that students understand and apply meaning. All learners must be engaged, with a variety of tasks offered within instruction as well as across students. Finally, there should be a balance between teacher-assigned and student-selected tasks, assuring that students have choices in their learning.

Differentiated instruction creates a flow in the classroom that you may not have experienced as a student. Tomlinson (1995) describes this flow as a movement from whole class work to independent, pair, or small group interaction, with a variety of materials, depending on student needs. The group then comes together to share before returning to their specific tasks. After a whole class review with the teacher, problems, cases, or activities are presented for student work. Students then return to the large group for mini-lessons in the skills that will later be needed to make presentations about the teacher-generated problems, cases, or activities. The group then breaks again, with students pursuing self-selected activities through which they will apply and extend their learning. The whole class comes together under the direction of the teacher to share individual study plans and establish how the products will be evaluated. This ebb and flow has several strengths. Students are engaged, provided choices, and have built-in opportunities to move about the room. The teacher has the opportunity to view students working with other students and demonstrating what they know about the concept.

Reflection

Consider your own experience when answering the questions below. Review your own experience as a student in terms of the "flow" described by Tomlinson (1995).

1. In what ways did your teachers use assessment as a teaching tool? Give examples.
2. How was assessment used to measure your learning? Give examples.

Instructional planning in culturally responsive classrooms is a complex task. However, teachers often feel more comfortable in terms of instruction than they do in terms of classroom management. In the next section, we will explore classroom management and climate in culturally responsive classrooms.

Differentiated Instruction
National Center on Accessing the General Curriculum
U.S. Office of Special Education Program: Ideas That Work

We are unique and the classroom is diverse. Differentiated instruction approaches learning so that students have multiple options for acquiring information and making sense of ideas. Differentiated learning requires flexibility, variety, and adjustment of curriculum and delivery to learners in contrast to the expectation that students modify themselves for the curriculum. The flexibility of instruction in the classroom uses a blend of whole group, group and individual instruction.

In one classroom, students express diversity in terms of background knowledge, readiness and language, and preferences in learning, interests, and responsiveness. The goal of a differentiated learning procedure would be to maximize each student's growth and individual success. The process assesses learners where they are and builds instruction from there. Content, process, and products are three key elements of differentiation (Tomlinson, 2001).

Content	Process	Products
Several elements and materials are used to support instructional content	**Flexible grouping is consistently used**	**Initial and on-going assessment of student readiness and growth are essential**
Includes: acts, concepts, generalizations or principles, attitudes, and skills. The variation seen in a differentiated classroom is most frequently the manner in which students gain access to important learning. Access to the content is key.	Expectations are that students will work together to develop knowledge of new content. Whole class intro discussions about big ideas followed by small group or pair work. Grouping is not fixed. Grouping and regrouping is a foundation of DL.	Pre-assessment leads to functional differentiation. Assessments include: interviews, surveys, performance, formal procedures. Assessment guides teachers to develop a menu of approaches, choices, scaffolds for varying needs, interests and abilities.
Align tasks and objects to learning goals	**Classroom management benefits students and teachers**	**Students are active and responsible explorers**
Objectives-driven menu makes it easier to find the next instructional step for learners entering at varying levels.	Consider organization and instructional delivery strategies to operate a classroom.	Each task placed before the learner will be interesting, engaging and accessible to essential understanding and skills. Each child feels challenged most of the time.
Instruction is concept-focused and principle driven	**GUIDELINES** Making differentiation possible • Clarify key concepts and generalizations • Use assessment as a teaching tool to extend versus merely measure instruction • Emphasize critical and creative thinking: understand & apply • Engaging all learners is essential: task variation • Provide a balance between teacher-assisted and student-selected tasks	**Vary expectations and requirements for student responses**
Concepts are broad based and not focused on minute details or unlimited facts. Teachers focus on the concepts, principles, and skills students should learn. Complexity is adjusted for diversity.		Items that students respond to are differentiated to demonstrate knowledge and understanding. Varied means of expression, procedure and difficulty, types of evaluation scoring.

Graphic organized by S. Kroeger, 2002

45

CHAPTER 3: CLASSROOM CLIMATE AND MANAGING BEHAVIOR

After completing this section, you will be able to:

- Discuss the importance of cooperative learning
- Explain a classroom climate that facilitates differentiated learning
- Describe a framework for constructing a positive and supportive environment for appropriate behavior

INTASC PRINCIPLES, KNOWLEDGE, DISPOSITIONS, AND PERFORMANCE

Principle 5: The teacher uses an understanding of individual and behavior to create a learning environment that encourages positive social interaction, active engagement in learning, and self-motivation

Knowledge:
- The teacher knows how to help people work productively and cooperatively with each other in complex social settings.
- The teacher recognizes factors and situations that are likely to promote or diminish intrinsic motivation, and knows how to help students become self-motivated.

Dispositions:
- The teacher takes responsibility for establishing a positive climate in the classroom and participates in maintaining such a climate in the school as a whole.
- The teacher values the role of students in promoting each other's learning and recognizes the importance of peer relationships in establishing a climate of learning.

Performances:
- The teacher creates a smoothly functioning learning community in which students assume responsibility for themselves and one another, participate in decision-making, work collaboratively and independently, and engage in purposeful learning activities.

Principle 6: The teacher uses knowledge of effective verbal, nonverbal, and media communication techniques to foster active inquiry, collaboration, and supportive interaction in the classroom.

Knowledge:
- The teacher understands how cultural and gender differences can affect communication in the classroom.

Performances:

- The teacher communicates in ways that demonstrate a sensitivity to cultural and gender differences (e.g., appropriate use of eye contact, interpretation of body language and verbal statements, and acknowledgement of and responsiveness to different modes of communication and participation).

COOPERATION AND CONSTRUCTIVE CONTROVERSY

Johnson and Johnson (2002) contend that the promise of diversity begins with establishing a learning community based on cooperation. *Community* is defined as a group of people who live in the same locality and share common goals and a common culture. Community includes all the stakeholders. A core behavior in a community is social interdependence. Social interdependence is evident when each individual's outcomes are affected by the actions of others. These outcomes can be positive or negative. The type of interdependence established significantly affects the outcomes of one's efforts to achieve higher levels of thinking, the quality of relationships and levels of cohesion, and the psychological adjustment leading to various levels of social competence. The authors outline some of the differences of the dynamics of social interdependence (Johnson & Johnson, 2002) as follows:

- *Cooperation*—individuals work together to achieve mutual goals. Individuals promote each other's success through assistance, support, encouragement, and a commitment to the common good. Success depends on joint efforts to achieve mutual goals. Encouragement is the natural interactive style. The pleasure of success is associated with the success of others. Others are seen as potential contributors. Differences are valued because of their unique contributions to the joint effort.

- *Competition*—individuals work against each other to achieve goals that only one or a few may attain. Individuals work to obstruct and block the efforts of others. There is a commitment to getting more than the others get. Success is defined as beating or defeating the other. Winning is more important than mastery of a skill. Sabotage is an implicitly accepted practice. The joy of winning is associated with another's defeat. Others are a threat to success. Those who are different are seen as threats if they have the advantage, but are ridiculed if they have a disadvantage.

- *Individualistic*—each person's outcomes are unaffected by any other's actions. In this context, people ignore each other's success or failure as they work alone. Success is dependent on your own effort and people are committed mainly to self-interest. The pleasure of success is private. Others are irrelevant.

The benefits of cooperative learning are numerous:

- cooperative learning ensures that all learners are meaningfully engaged.

- students will reach their full potential and experience success that further motivates investment of energy and effort.

- promotion of caring and committed relationships among students.

- development of interpersonal and small group skills such as leadership, decision making, and problem-solving.

- provides a context in which personal problems can be shared and resolved.

- cooperative groups promote a sense of pride and willingness to assist one another (Johnson & Johnson, 2002).

The skills and values of cooperation are tested during constructive conflict resolution procedures. When conflicts are resolved successfully, increased levels of energy and insight result. Other outcomes include development of cognitive and social skills, as well as strengthening of relationships.

Resolving conflicts successfully requires access to clear procedures that are taught in a school climate that supports the use of such procedures. Without procedural skills and supportive school-wide values, conflict can destroy relationships. Johnson and Johnson (2002) discuss one exercise where students purposefully engage in an academic controversy. A controversy exists when you have two incompatible positions and the individuals with the opposing views need to reach an agreement.

Students are randomly assigned to heterogeneous groups of four. The groups are assigned to give a report upon which they will be tested. Each group is divided into pairs. One pair takes a *pro* position and the other takes the *con* position. Materials to define the positions are supplied, as well as sources for further research. Each group is to reach a consensus by synthesizing the best information from both sides. The process has five steps:

- research, learn, and prepare positions.

- present and advocate the position.

- engage in an open discussion in which there is spirited disagreement.

- reverse positions and present the best case.

- synthesize; at this step all advocacy is dropped and finding a synthesis is paramount.

- evaluation of performance (Johnson & Johnson, 2002).

Problem solving negotiations focus on resolving differences constructively. A conflict of interest exists when the actions of one person attempt to maximize his or her wants and interests and at the same time block or interfere with the wants and needs of another person. Negotiations may be categorized as distributive or integrative. In distributive (or win-lose) negotiations, one person benefits only if the other agrees to a concession, ending in destructive consequences for the relationship. In integrative (or problem solving) negotiations, parties to the disagreement work together to create an agreement from which both benefit, ending in a constructive outcome. There are six steps in the integrative approach:

- describing what you want.

- describing how you feel.

- describing the reasons for your wants and feelings.

- taking the other person's perspective and summarizing that perspective.

- inventing three optional plans to resolve the conflict that maximize joint benefits.

- choosing one of the options with a formal agreement or a handshake.

The benefits of integrative conflict resolution include the development of a common language for negotiation. Attitudes toward conflict improve when participants see themselves as winners.

The procedures of negotiation are learned. Students tend to generalize the skills and use them independently. Conflict resolution procedures and values tend to support school-wide values and priorities. When teachers integrated these procedures into the academic context, long-term retention improved and academic achievement increased (Johnson & Johnson, 2002).

Civic Values

Civic values are common goals that increase the quality of life within a community. Civic values tend to favor cooperation and de-emphasize competition and individualism. Civic values are aspects of the hidden curriculum of a school and they can be directly taught, role played, and assigned as special roles in the school culture. Faculty members model civic values and use them in daily practice.

Cooperation, constructive controversy, and civic values can help build the creative energy of a culturally responsive classroom and support the democratic values of the U.S. Constitution and Bill of Rights. These same values can de-emphasize prejudice and ethnocentrism. As the complexity and diversity of the classroom increase, skills in cooperation, constructive controversy, and civic values enhance the process of building a vibrant community. They are life-long skills that will be useful in settings and situations far beyond the classroom (Johnson & Johnson, 2002).

As we build a culturally responsive classroom, educators and families are invited to think critically about the resources we need to complete the task and the ways in which we need to change in order to respond to diversity.

Reflection

Consider your own experience when answering the questions below. Teaching standards suggest that educators value the role of students in promoting each other's learning and recognizes the importance of peer relationships in establishing a climate of learning.

1. Consider the scope of a school year and explain the various stages of development you would want to see students move through with regard to cooperative learning skills
2. What measures would you use to determine whether your goals were being met?

COOPERATION AND CRITICAL THINKING SKILLS

Cooperative learning makes sense in inclusive classrooms because it builds on heterogeneity and formalizes and encourages peer support and connection (Sapon-Shevin, Ayres, & Duncan, 2002).. Sapon-Shevin (1998) examined one K-6 environment where teachers used a more system-wide approach to inclusion. These teachers knew that mere physical inclusion would not guarantee social inclusion. They saw that children with disabilities, as well as students from other marginalized groups, continued to be isolated from the rest of the learning community. Even when there were plans to establish supportive friendships, they noticed these relationships tended to lack reciprocity. The child with the "difference" was on the receiving end. Following Paley's lead, a group of teachers implemented a new rule: "You can't say you can't play" (Paley, 1992). The experiment allowed teachers to see that they could alter the social patterns of student interactions by approaching the environment systematically. By focusing on social climate, rather than the child, positive changes occurred for everyone (Sapon-Shevin, 1998).

Sapon-Shevin (1994) defined cooperative learning as a way of organizing instruction that involves students working together to help one another learn. Students must serve as each other's resources in order to be successful. Turning Points (1989) identifies cooperative learning as a key strategy of success for all students (Sapon-Shevin, 1994).

Why is cooperative learning so popular in middle school? Sapon-Shevin (1994) points to a number of reasons for its attractiveness:

- an uncanny match between cooperative learning and adolescent learning needs.

- creation of democratic, inclusive institutions, not tracking on basis of class, race, or gender, is highly compatible with cooperative learning.

- reduces the teasing and taunting that occur in the middle school—within a team, cooperation is required for success.

- leads to increased achievement and better attitudes and self-esteem.

- simple and easy to implement.

However, Sapon-Shevin (1994) contends that students may lack the skills needed for the demands of cooperation. Cooperative learning cannot be implemented independent of other reforms. When competition, tracking, and exclusion are widespread, the culture of the school sends a different message. Without critical evaluation of how school culture is structured, the inherent contradictions may create significant inhibitors. Tracking and democracy are contradictory. If the gifted feel used, or the children with disabilities feel like scapegoats, maybe deeper issues need to be addressed.

Cooperative learning can be threatening to teachers for the following reasons:

- control and predictability are reduced.

- attention to social goals is required.

- our commitment to individualism is challenged.

- our commitment to the value of competition is challenged.

Cooperative learning may be a form of norm switching. For example, a teacher may be in complete control of the environment most of the day, and then for 45 minutes have to cooperate. Cooperative learning, however, insists that we pay attention to the norm of student empowerment throughout the day. Teachers must feel empowered. If they do not feel empowered, they will not be able to empower children. Administrative support is critical. Teachers need time to meet, share with, learn from, and support one another (Sapon-Shevin, 1994).

The focus on social goals varies widely from school to school. Some teach explicit social skills and conflict resolution while others simply consider focus on social goals to be a vehicle to academic achievement. Social skills training requires:

- education of teachers to teach social skills.

- curricular goals that include social skills.

- evaluation of social skills through ongoing assessment.

Sapon-Shevin (1994) contends that a focus on community is key for the success of cooperative learning. Just to learn better social skills to get a better job does nothing to challenge the individualism at the core of American education or society. Have we failed, she asks, to communicate the value of diversity, respect and inclusion? Substituting homogeneous for the heterogeneous is a failure of the process. Rotating membership frequently fails to address bias and prejudice.

If this change does not occur, we are merely tinkering at the edge. In fact, we may be simply recreating existing race, class, and gender inequalities in our society. Cooperative learning requires a school-wide philosophy. School staff and leadership need to think critically to uncover and dismantle structures and procedures that work against community formation and make room for equity and justice.

Sapon-Shevin (2001) discusses the growing diversity of our society. For example:

- one in three students is a racial or ethnic minority.

- by 2020, 46 percent of the student population will be students of color.

- by 2035, this group will constitute a numerical majority.

- by 1995, 2.5 percent of students spoke English as a second language.

- 1 in 5 students under 18 live in poverty.

- Fewer than 50 percent of students live with a biological parent.

- 59 percent of our students will live in a single parent household.

- 6–14 million children live in a household headed by gay or lesbian family members.

- 10–20 percent of school age youth self-identify as gay or lesbian.

- 1–2 percent of children are adopted.

- inclusion has brought hundreds of thousands of students identified as disabled into the classroom, students who were previously served in separate programs, separate schools, or completely unserved.

Sapon-Shevin (2001) contends that there was never such a thing as a homogeneous classroom—our classrooms have always been diverse. The author sees the bifurcation of teacher preparation as impeding our ability to think critically about issues of diversity. The author proposes that if teachers visualize what might-be, then they make the what-is intolerable. Teachers can value multiple identities and avoid the slippery slope of partial inclusion. Differences are natural, inevitable, and desirable, enriching teaching and learning experiences. For example, as educators we can conceptualize disability as a social construct, closely linked to cultural, political, and economic demands and limitations (Sapon-Shevin, 2001).

In a culturally responsive school, diversity is not viewed as an add-on. Sapon-Shevin (2001) suggests we ask ourselves these critical questions about the educational environment and climate:

- How is curriculum structured? For example, do we incorporate differentiated instruction and knowledge of multiple intelligences?

- How is diversity represented? Can we account for some parents who might be in jail, deceased, or in employment they are not comfortable talking about?

- How is assessment diverse?

- Do teachers model respect for diversity?

- Are we utilizing the benefits of peer tutoring without having one person stuck permanently in the role of receiving help?

- Is reciprocity one of our core values?

- Is our goal is not to make differences invisible (as if the differences were negative qualities), or do we have an explicit way to respect and learn from the differences in our school culture (Sapon-Shevin, 2001)?

As we carefully and critically consider the professional development needs of the culturally responsive classroom, the awareness of the specific aspects and characteristics of cooperative learning become more focused. Educators must begin to utilize the intelligences and skills found in every member of the learning environment.

Reflection

Consider your own experience when answering the question below. Teachers can be quickly overwhelmed with the needs of the immediate environment. Time for critical reflection and consideration of one's teaching stance can dim in the pressure to have class ready for the next morning

1. What are some practical ways you can ensure that you will have time to critically consider your role as a professional educator during the school year?

COOPERATIVE LEARNING FOR FUTURE ORIENTATIONS

Kagan (1994) states that in the process of teaching others, we learn more. As the old saying goes, "when you teach, you learn twice" (Kagan, 1998). When an individual has to present information or a process, rather than listen to someone else present, the information takes on a fresh quality and the teacher/tutor learns in more depth. Peer tutors make substantial academic gains, as well as developing leadership skills and conflict resolution skills. The great strength of cooperative learning is that the process utilizes the interpersonal intelligences of the students (Kagan, 1994).

The largest and fastest growing segment of the U. S. economy is the information sector, which involves generating, analyzing, and communicating knowledge. Increasingly, the norm of the workplace is interactive teams that solve problems using critical thinking skills. It is possible that half of the kindergarten students of today will be in jobs that do not yet exist. Cooperative teamwork and communication will characterize the workplace of the future. The heterogeneous team in the classroom is a microcosm of our society for now and in the future. The skills needed for cooperative work and collaboration are increasingly important. When we consider the aspects of U.S. society that place children at risk for failure, giving students access to problem solving skills and cooperative learning become protective factors in the learning environment. Cooperative learning methods, which assume heterogeneity, are better designed to cope with the diversity of today's students.

In a cooperative learning environment, students choose more friends from other races and interact in a more integrated pattern. Kagan (1994) points out that in numerous cooperative learning environments, a dramatic reduction or elimination of self-segregation follows even brief cooperative learning experiences. When students are allowed to work together they experience an increase in a variety of social skills such as problem solving and taking the role of the other, as welling as increased willingness to help others.

Kagan (1994) outlines six key concepts of cooperative learning

- Heterogeneous teams, when carefully formed, frequently consist of small numbers that endure over a period. The diversity of the team reflects the classroom. Teams provide opportunities for peer tutoring, and improve cross culture and cross gender integration. Heterogeneous teams can be thoughtfully designed using a ranking sheet that lists students according to achievement and then selecting from the high, middle and low ranks to create the team.

- Cooperative learning ensures equal and easy access to other team members and materials. Teams make use of frequent modeling and have established class rules and norms for team functioning.

- The will to cooperate is supported through the use of team building and class building that encourage trust and respect. Clear tasks and rewards are integral to cooperative learning. Jigsaw tasks that require each member to contribute help build the will to cooperate. Rewards do not single out ability levels, which creates discouragement. Rewards are also designed to support the entire class to avoid inter-team rivalry. Between-team cooperative tasks can be designed for such purposes.

- The skills needed to cooperate will depend on the complexity of the assigned task. Problem solving skills, conflict resolution, and agenda revision can all be modeled and role-played in an environment that reinforces these methods.

- Three basic principles of cooperative learning include simultaneous interaction, positive interdependence, and individual accountability.

  o Simultaneous interaction dramatically increases response time in contrast to sequential interaction. In a traditional classroom, the teacher does 80 percent of the talking. In teams, all the students are discussing the plans in pairs and search for information to solve a problem at the same time. When a student asks for help, it is received immediately.

  o Positive interdependence means that the gain of one student is the gain of the others. Movement to a next stage can be contingent on everyone reaching a certain level. This creates the motivation to assist all learners to reach the required stage.

  o Individual accountability is an integral aspect of cooperative learning. Color code individual contributions or average the teams test scores. Use talking chips. Use paraphrasing or "I heard from" statements. Use a three-step interview where students first discuss in pairs, then reverse roles, and finally, share with the group what they learned in the interview. The Think-Pair-Share sequences can stimulate participation.

- Structures will vary according to learning objectives and content.

These skills and procedures of the cooperative learning classroom are supported from many directions in the literature and research. One thing is clear: we must prepare ourselves to become effective collaborators in this process of creating a culturally responsive classroom. Putnam (1998, p.17) explains that appropriate instructional approaches must be in place in order to preempt the breakdown in learning and morale that can sometimes result when classroom demographics and student learning needs begin to change and the instructional method remain the same.

Reflection

Consider your own experience when answering the questions below. The teaching standards indicate that teachers recognize factors and situations that are likely to promote or diminish intrinsic motivation, and know how to help students become self-motivated. Cooperative learning skills may offer specific ways to encourage intrinsic motivation in the classroom.

1. In your own experience, how has intrinsic motivation developed in your life as a learner?

2. What are the conditions or circumstances that facilitate intrinsic motivation for you?

3. What are the barriers to the development of intrinsic motivation?

COOPERATIVE LEARNING PROCESS

Putnam (1998) is convinced that the movement from tracking and homogeneous instructional groupings to diverse heterogeneous (cooperative) groupings must be linked with appropriate modifications in teaching techniques. The positive results and high achievements that are outcomes of cooperative learning groups occur only under conditions in which there is support, training, and regular use of the methods (Putnam, 1998).

Positive interdependence is an aspect of cooperative learning in which that the gain of one student is the gain of the others. Movement to a next stage can be contingent on everyone reaching a certain level. This creates the motivation to assist all learners to reach the required stage (Kagan, 1994). Putnam (1998) called positive interdependence the essence of cooperative learning. Students begin to think in terms of "we" instead of "me." There are several methods for achieving positive interdependence:

- mutual goal interdependence.

- task interdependence that involves the division of labor and different roles.

- resource interdependence that requires sharing among participants.

- reward interdependence for achievement.

Individual accountability is an integral aspect of cooperative learning. Use of Think-Pair-Share sequences enhances accountability. Putnam (1998) contends that these methods discourage hitchhiking and coasting. Random selection of students for short reports and self-monitoring sheets also support participation from all group members.

Individual Accountability Self-Monitoring Form

Name   Group Name
Date   Subject

Did I contribute to the group work today? Yes   No
How?

Did I reach my own learning goal today? Yes   No
My learning goal was

What I accomplished:

Is there anything that I could do to improve my accountability?

My future accountability goal is:

The cooperative skills needed to complete an assignment should be demonstrated and practiced with accompanying feedback of performance. Skills for sharing materials, active listening, encouraging, and problem solving will vary from task to task and within age groups. Putnam (1998) encourages the use of T-charts to help the group define and understand the skills being taught. For example, the following table is an example of a T-chart developed with fifth graders (Putnam, 1998).

Social Skill: Praising Others	
Sounds like	**Looks like**
Good job	Smiling
Fantastic	Thumbs up
Yes!	High-five
I like your idea	Leaning forward
Wicked good	Pat on the back
Super	Nodding head

Face-to-face interaction that includes verbal and nonverbal communication is preferred over interactions with a machine or materials. When students work independently, they meet in groups to discuss answers.
.

Student reflection and goal setting exercises are critical to develop opportunities for self-praise and evaluation. Putnam (1998) offers the following sheet as an example.

Cooperative Group Reflection and Goal Setting

Group Name: Date:

How well did our group:	Needs Improvement	Good	Excellent
1. Complete the task?			
2. Use time wisely?			
3. Practice the social skill?			

What we did especially well:

What we need to improve on:

Future goal(s):

Equal opportunity for success depends on student needs. When a cooperative learning experience is unsuccessful for either an individual or a group, carefully analyze the process according to the above characteristics. Problem solve your next experiences with knowledge you have gained from previous cooperative learning exercises.

Putnam (1998, p. 43) offers a strategy card as a way to help support student preparation and participation in a cooperative learning exercise.

Strategy Card

When I am in a group activity, I work with group members to discuss information, solve a problem, or work on a project. I am a valuable member of the group.

1. Before beginning
   a. **Do I understand** the directions and the goal of the group activity?
2. If I do not understand the directions or the goal of the activity, **I ask the group members.** If they do not know, I ask the teacher to explain the directions or goals again.
3. Every few minutes I ask myself
   a. **Am I listening** to the group members?
   b. **Am I helping** in some way to complete the group activity?
4. At the end if the activity, I complete the sentence
   a. **I learned that…**

Brain research (Gardner, 1993) continues to assist teachers in the construction of culturally responsive classrooms. Students, regardless of their backgrounds or ages, come to the classroom as diverse learners who have preferences and interests that have been developed and sparked by the various experiences of their lives. An understanding of the multiple intelligences can enhance a teacher's repertoire of skills and approaches to the diverse classroom.

TEACHING THE SKILLS OF INTELLIGENCE

Once a learner recognizes strength in his or her intellect, and that strength is celebrated, the successful experience may lead to development of other strengths (Kagan, 1998).

Consider the case history of Paula (Kagan, 1998). Early in school, Paula was assessed as having learning disabilities; she developed low self-esteem and a dislike for school. By the fifth grade, she was several grade levels behind her classmates. Paula attempted suicide in the summer before entering sixth grade. Paula's sixth grade teacher noticed that Paula moved with poise and dignity. Following her hunch that Paula would benefit from kinesthetic instruction, the teacher asked Paula to create a movement alphabet—movements to form the letters of the alphabet. Paula responded positively and created a sequenced dance that mastered the alphabet as well as complete sentences that she then performed before the class. Paula rapidly improved her reading and by the end of the sixth grade was reading at grade level, fully included and receiving above average grades. A shift in instructional strategy was required, using kinesthetic rather than verbal sequential learning. Recognizing and celebrating Paula's strength in the area of movement led to the development of strengths in many other areas of intelligence.

Kagen (1998) suggests that educators enhance instruction with the multiple intelligences as a way to maximize academic success. By matching intelligence and instruction, we increase opportunities for individuals to reach goals appropriate to them. Kagan (1998) suggests several ideas in each intelligence area.

- *Verbal/l\Linguistic and the Telephone*—From a group of four, one student leaves. The rest of the team receives instructions. They listen carefully because they know they will have to deliver the instructions to someone else. The team will receive the grade that the student who was outside receives when quizzed on the content. Regardless of the academic content, Telephone develops listening skills, as well as descriptive oral language.

- *Mathematical/Logical and Find My Rule*—Find My Rule is a concept development structure; it develops inductive reasoning. Teams try to find the rule while the teacher adds items to a graphic organizer on the board. Once a team thinks it has found the rule the members test it at the board or projector.

- *Visual/Spatial and Team Mind Map*—Also referred to as a word-web or spider map, the process develops visual and spatial relationships among ideas. Working on a big sheet of paper with markers, team members draw a central idea in the middle. Using a round table motif, the teams draw connections to main ideas. Connecting ideas are then added in a free-for-all.

- *Bodily/Kinesthetic and Formations*—Students move to form bodily representations of a symbol, object, or system, such as a math equation or a science concept.

- *Musical/Rhythmic and Songs and Poems for Two Voices*—Each student is an "A" or a "B" and sings lines when a script calls for his or her participation. Students eventually develop their own songs and poems using the Two Voices method.

- *Interpersonal/Social and the Team Interview*—A teammate is interviewed by three teammates at once and acts three times in the role of the interviewer, each for 1-2 minute intervals. For example, you could ask, "If you could invent something that would help people what would it be?" Follow-up questions would draw out more reasoning.

- *Intrapersonal/Introspective and Visualize Share*—The teacher leads a visualization exercise to bring students into contact with feelings and goals. They can visit historical places or part of the body, or they are asked to see themselves as successful at some task.

- *Naturalist and Same/Different*—This exercise develops skills in comparing and contrasting by finding subtle differences among flora, fauna, and other content represented visually or in tone. Usually completed in pairs, pictures will have 20 differences, some obvious and others more subtle.

Developing the multiple intelligences allows for celebration of growth and discovery. The use of multiple intelligences is a logical link to the differentiated classroom, which attempts to increase access to the curriculum. When asked about the definition of being smart, Gardner (1993) replied that being smart means having the ability to solve problems, create new problems to solve, and create products and services of value in at least some culture. By widening the definition, the meaning of intelligence becomes more inclusive. Thinking creatively can enhance the culturally responsive classroom (Kagan, 1998). (Tables that outline the intelligences and criteria for identifying them are on the following pages.)

In addition to the intellectual diversity found in every classroom, we can also consider behavioral diversity. Behavior in particular interacts with the learning environment in significant ways. Our awareness of how a classroom and school environment interacts with the behaviors in that environment constitutes a huge step forward in the design of a culturally responsive classroom.

Multiple Intelligences (Gardner, 1993)

VISUAL/SPATIAL	VERBAL/LINGUISTIC	MATHEMATICAL/LOGICAL
VISUAL/SPATIAL Children who learn best visually and organize things spatially. They like to see what you are talking about in order to understand. They enjoy charts, graphs, maps, tables, illustrations, art, puzzles, costumes—anything eye catching ("picture smart")	**VERBAL/LINGUISTIC** Children who demonstrate strength in the language arts: speaking, writing, reading, listening. These students have always been successful in traditional classrooms because their intelligence lends itself to traditional teaching. ("word smart")	**MATHEMATICAL/LOGICAL** Children who display an aptitude for numbers, reasoning, and problem solving. This is the other half of the children who typically do well in traditional classrooms where teaching is logically sequenced and students are asked to conform. ("number/reasoning smart")
BODILY/KINESTHETIC Children who experience learning best through activity: games, movement, hands-on tasks, building. These children were often labeled "overly active" in traditional classrooms, where they were told to sit and be still! ("body smart")	**MUSICAL/RHYTHMIC** Children who learn well through songs, patterns, rhythms, instruments, and musical expression. It is easy to overlook children with this intelligence in traditional education. ("music smart")	**INTRAPERSONAL** Children who are especially in touch with their own feelings, values and ideas. They may tend to be reserved, but they are actually quite intuitive about what they learn and how it relates to them. ("self smart")
INTERPERSONAL Children who are noticeably people oriented and outgoing, and do their learning cooperatively in groups or with a partner. These children may have typically been identified as "talkative" or "too concerned about being social" in a traditional setting. ("people smart")	**NATURALIST** Children who love the outdoors, animals, field trips. More than this, though, these students love to pick up on subtle differences in meanings. The traditional classroom has not been accommodating to these children. ("nature smart")	**EXISTENTIALIST** Children who learn in the context of where humankind stands in the "big picture" of existence. They ask "Why are we here?" and "What is our role in the world?" This intelligence is seen in the discipline of philosophy. ("metaphysical smart")

Howard Gardner developed the theory of multiple intelligences in 1983.
Source: http://www.thomasarmstrong.com/multiple_intelligences.htm &
http://surfaquarium.com/mi.htm [Table organization by S. Kroeger]

Isolation as a Brain Function	Evolutionary History	Supported Psychometric Tasks
As medicine studies isolated brain functions through cases of brain injury and degenerative disease, we are able to identify actual physiological locations for specific brain functions. A true intelligence will have its function identified in a specific location in the human brain.	As cultural anthropologists continue to study the history of human evolution, there is adequate evidence that our species has developed intelligence over time through human experience. A true intelligence can have its development traced through the evolution of *homo sapiens*.	The use of psychometric instruments to measure intelligence (such as I.Q. tests) has traditionally been used to measure only specific types of ability. However, these tests can be designed and used to identify and quantify true unique intelligences. The Multiple Intelligence theory does not reject psychometric testing for specific scientific study.
Developmental History with an Expert End Performance	**Gardner's Eight Criteria**	**Prodigies, Idiot Savants, and Exceptional Individuals**
As clinical psychologists continue to study the developmental stages of human growth and learning, a clear pattern of development is being documented for the human mind. A true intelligence has an identifiable set of stages of growth with a Mastery Level, which exists as an end state in human development. We can see examples of people who have reached the Mastery level for each intelligence.	For Identifying an Intelligence (1983) "Intelligence is the ability to find and solve problems and create products of value in one's own culture." 1. Everyone has ALL the intelligences 2. The intelligences are not mutually exclusive—they act in consort 3. MI Theory was not developed to exclude individuals, but to allow all people to contribute to society through their own strengths.	Human record of genius such as Mozart being able to perform on the piano at the age of four and Dustin Hoffman's "Rainman" character being able to calculate dates accurately down to the day of the week indicate that there are specific human abilities that can demonstrate themselves to high degrees in unique cases. Highly developed examples of a true intelligence are recorded in rare occurrences.
Supported Psychological Tasks	**Set of Core Operations**	**Encoded in a Symbol System**
Clinical psychologists can identify sets of tasks for different domains of human behavior. A true intelligence can be identified by specific tasks, which can be carried out, observed, and measured.	There is an identifiable set of procedures and practices that is unique to each of the intelligences.	Humans have developed many kinds of symbol systems over time for varied disciplines. A true intelligence has its own set of images it uses which are unique to itself and are important in completing its identified set of tasks.

REGULARITY CONTROL: AFFECTING CLASSROOM BEHAVIOR

According to Coombs-Richardson and Meisgeier (2001), the classroom environment, routines, rules, teaching methods, physical arrangements, and the overall climate of the classroom are an expression of an educator's teaching stance. In conjunction with school-wide policies, they form what are called classroom *regularities*. Regularities occur with consistency and in routine ways and create predictability in the school day (Coombs-Richardson & Meisgeier, 2001).

Coombs-Richardson and Meisgeier (2001) indicate that it is important to recognize behavioral diversity in a classroom and to establish flexible regularities. The classroom environment, routines, rules, teaching methods, homework expectations, test types, dress code, educational stance, and physical arrangements all constitute behavioral antecedents. Antecedents are arrangements in the classroom or school environment that exist before the behavior occurs. They form the conditions that prompt the behavior in the first place. They also constitute the likelihood that the behavior will occur again. Some antecedents exist in the home or community. Educators need to be fully aware of the regularities in their classrooms in order to design effective behavior management. Regularities will vary from classroom to classroom, depending on the teacher.

The most important variables in the management of appropriate classroom behavior seem to be associated with the following:

- establishing and reinforcing reasonable rules and routines that support the on-task behavior intended to master instructional objectives.

- a teacher's ability to develop and use a variety of interventions diverse enough to accommodate many kinds of situations and student personality types, interests, and intelligences.

- a teacher's ability to assess classroom climate, recognize potential problems in order to avoid them, modify classroom regularities, and have at his or her fingertips a wide array of behavioral interventions.

- teachers who have positive interpersonal relationships with their students and a classroom where students feel physically and psychologically safe.

- teachers who are themselves life-long learners, who consistently strive to provide a healthy environment in which children can take risks and fail safely and can learn and grow physically, psychologically, socially, and academically.

Regularities that contribute to behavioral problems can be changed once they are recognized. Coombs-Richardson and Meisgeier (2001) have identified several steps to help teachers develop effective discipline practices:

- *Establish regularity control*—Coombs-Richardson and Meisgeier (2001) suggest that as soon as a class of students is established, the regularities that influence classroom operations should be identified. Identify which regularities are controllable (changeable) by teachers or school officials, and which regularities are incontrollable (unchangeable). Identify those that influence instruction and student performance and those that influence social interactions and behavior. Establish priorities for how to alter or change your classroom and begin to monitor the effect of any change you make.

- *Help students and teachers accept responsibility*—Empowering students in the process of developing a learning community is critical. Using metacognitive skills, cognitive behavior modification, self-reinforcement, self-management, and problem-solving to increase self-control and assuming responsibility for one's own learning can contribute significantly to the learning process.

- *Provide a variety of instructional arrangements*—The use of differentiated instructional arrangement can assist in the learning process. Neuroscience suggests that intense focus on new materials is limited to a short time. Using such methods as mastery learning, continuous progress learning, personalized instruction, families, cohorts, or school within school may be beneficial.

- *Expect good behavior with good performance*—It is a mistake to separate problem behaviors from academic effort and success. Academic success may be the most significant anecdote to a problem behavior. Students often make helpful partners in the problem solving process.

- *Adopt a positive attitude*—When students are not doing well, it is well known that teachers also experience significant discouragement. When faced with the difficulty in classroom behavior management, remember that it is a problem waiting to be solved, not a sign of failure.

- *Establish positive emotional regularities*—When learners do not feel safe in a classroom they will downshift to a flight, fight, or freeze response that results in the need for intensive intervention. Establishing a classroom that is safe, respectful and supportive creates conditions for learning and retention of new information.

- *Plan for effective management*—A warm and encouraging classroom, with brisk and continuous pace of instruction, and discipline procedures that are fair and equitable will be fertile ground for cooperative learning and shared responsibility.

SETTING EVENTS AND ESTABLISHING OPERATIONS

The regularities referred to above are closely related to what are called setting events, or establishing operations. Setting events increase or decrease the probability of interactions between a teacher and student or a student and peers. The environment is complex and some behaviors result from multiple causes, but contingencies can combine to make a behavior more likely or less likely to occur. For example, when you are thirsty, finding water becomes very important. The biblical story of Esau selling his birthright to Jacob for a simple drink of water is a classic example of the power of a setting event (Genesis 25:29–34). Interventions are designed to neutralize a setting event/establishing operation, but the setting events must first be identified (Fox, 1990; Kantor, 1970; Mayer, 1995; McGill, 1999; Michael, 2000; Wilder & Carr, 1998).

Setting events are important to understanding behaviors. Take the example of Kelly Kennedy & Itkonen, 1993). Traveling in a motor vehicle was initially identified as problematic for Kelly. It turns out it was when the vehicle made frequent stops that her behavior became problematic. As long as the vehicle was moving, no problem behaviors occurred. One route had 20 stops (city streets), but the highway route had only two stops. The setting event intervention consisted of the aide who drove Kelly not being assigned the 20-stop route, but using only the highway route.

Setting events may also be at work with teachers. The coercive cycle can be common in the classroom. A history of negative teacher-student interactions for a student may be one contributing factor to truancy and dropout. While teacher attention (teacher praise) has been proven effective, the lower the social development of a child, the less frequent the praise they receive, creating a negative cycle. In one study, a teacher gave forty-five disapproval statements for every three praise statements in an hour. Why do the negatives win? The effect of a negative statement is immediate and reciprocal. However, the long-term effects may be detrimental. Shores and associates studied four classroom management strategies as setting events for teacher/student interaction. They found that rules regulate behavior by clearly defining expectations. They observed that classroom arrangements such as cubicles, small groups, and space between students give teachers a competitive advantage. The study also noted that external reinforcers, like token and point economies, are very successful. While they may increase the rate of teacher praise, they may also increase negative interactions when the system is not working. All of these strategies may be setting events for either coercive or reciprocal interaction. Just overhearing teacher lunchroom conversations indicates that the negative side of the interaction tends to reign in many classrooms. When do we hear, for example, "I put Jimmy's desk next to mine to I can reinforce his appropriate behavior more often?" (Shores, Gunter, & Jack, 1993).

Setting events let us know that there is more going on than meets the eye. Seventeen-year-old Terri demonstrated periodic verbal and physical outbursts (Dadson & Horner, 1993). A functional behavioral assessment identified seven events as likely to affect Terri's problem behaviors and seven behaviors considered problematic. The team met with the family to determine the relative importance of each one. A baseline was gathered for forty-five days. The results of the baseline and analysis showed that two setting events, late bus and poor sleep, were associated with the targeted behaviors.

The intervention for Terri included the following: first, the family would call the school whenever either of the setting events, late bus or poor sleep, occurred. The school responded by having the teaching assistant meet Terri at the bus and deliver praise for specific behaviors. Early in the school day Terri was allowed to choose a teaching assistant to work with on a one-to-one. Terri was given a choice to skip calisthenics and do stretching instead. Finally, on days the setting events occurred, the staff increased Terri's opportunities to choose the order of tasks she would perform. These interventions proved successful (Dadson & Horner, 1993).

Most teachers know that setting events affect the behavior of children—what they have not had is an effective way to use that information. Often behaviors seem "out of the blue" and some days are "bad days." Behaviors include: screaming, hitting, biting, pulling hair, hitting self, eating, smoking, throwing objects, scratching, grabbing, whining, crying, resisting, spitting, lacking self-restraint, pulling away, walking away, breaking, and dropping on the floor. The function of many of these is avoidance or escape. Setting events are legion. They include such things as illness, injury, pain, constipation, awake at night and left in room, staff change, loud noise, outing denied, schedule change, lost game, a fight on the bus, agitation, lack of sleep, fatigue, hunger, and aggression (Horner, Vaughn, Day, & Ard, 1996).

Horner and associates state that effective behavioral interventions typically involve changing existing environments in a manner that makes problem behaviors irrelevant, ineffective, and inefficient (Norner et al., 1996). The assumption behind setting event manipulation is that there are stable and effective multileveled interventions already in place. However, setting events decrease their effectiveness. The authors suggest five responses:

- minimize the likelihood of setting event; get more sleep if tiredness is the problem.

- neutralize effect of setting event; if a child was just in an argument and is agitated, provide time to relax—build neutralizing routines such as the Brain Gym (Dennison & Dennison, 1989; Hannaford, 1995).

- withhold the stimulus; change the task to an easier one and ease into the tougher one.

- add a prompt for the desired behavior; for example, "If you need help with this, ask for it, tell me."

- increase the value of consequences for desired behaviors; increase opportunities for immediate praise.

In their discussion of classroom regularities, Coombs-Richardson and Meisgeier (2001) compare traditional classroom regularities with alternative classroom regularities. In the traditional model one has a sense of the classroom based on a factory model and in the alternate classroom model, a more authentic real-world picture emerges.

Coombs-Richardson and Meisgeier (2001) describe the traditional classroom regularity, in which time slots for various content areas tend to be more constant. Seats are in orderly rows and students must raise their hands to speak. In the traditional model, teachers do the teaching and students speak only to answer questions. There may be an assumption that some students want to learn and some do not or cannot. Compliance with classroom rules is assured though intimidation and punishment. In this traditional model, assessment is formal, traditional, and norm-referenced. Students move from grade to grade, year by year.

In contrast, the alternate classroom regularity uses block scheduling and students work at tables or in centers. Students learn a system of self-regulation for order, and ask questions, as well as answering them. In the alternate classroom regularity, instruction includes a variety of resources and activities that involve hands-on projects or role-plays. Teachers work together to create interdisciplinary units of learning. Teachers assume that all students can learn and permit some students to develop their own learning plans. The teacher works to create a friendly, supportive, cooperative, and safe learning climate. Assessment in the alternate classroom is informal, curriculum-based, and criterion referenced, or includes work samples in portfolios. Students move within families, houses, or cohorts when ready (Coombs-Richardson and Meisgeier, 2001).

Reflection

Consider your own experience when answering the questions below. Educators are expected to know how to help people work productively and cooperatively with each other in complex social settings.

1. Can you think of reasons why a certain social setting might work well one day but not on another day?
2. How would you go about creating a flexible learning plan to accommodate such an occurrence?

WHAT IF THE PROBLEM PERSISTS?

There are times when the teacher is faced with difficult classroom behaviors that are persistent and resist change. Insight into cultural differences and priorities of families can help teachers in designing management plans that have a better fit for the individual (Horner, 1997; Parette & Petch-Hogan, 2001; Vaughn, Dunlap, Fox, Clarke, & Bucy, 1997). When families are included, and have accepted ownership of the interventions that they helped create, the intervention has a broader base of acceptance (Lesar, Trivette, & Dunst, 1995; Rock, 2000; Skinner, Bailey, Correa, & Rodriguez, 1999). With family involvement, seeing the situation from the child's point of view is more likely to include comprehensive elements of the child's life (Smith, 1989).

The failure of educators to learn and develop effective educational knowledge and strategies stands in the way of every child receiving a first-class education in America. Particularly at risk of not receiving needed and timely instructional and related services are those youth who are significantly impacted by social, emotional, and/or behavioral problems, including children with significant mental health needs *(In the best interests of all: A position paper of the children's behavioral alliance*, 2003; Wolfensberger, 1972).

Increasing numbers of students and their families are affected by environmental and interpersonal risk factors that may interfere with the student's basic needs and ability to learn. Poverty, divorce, pregnancy, single parents, abuse and neglect, serious illnesses, suicide, and homelessness are all potential risk factors children face.(Heaviside et al., 1998; Katz, 1997; Keogh & Weisner, 1993; Masten, Best, & Garmezy, 1990; Masten, Morison, Pellegrini, & Tellegen, 1990; Meyer, Mitchell, Clementii, & Clement-Robertson, 1993; Prater, Sileo, & Black, 2000).

Today's inclusive classroom is a more complex learning environment than classrooms of 20 years ago. Teachers report that behavior management is an area of critical need, but receives little attention. Teachers often find themselves feeling confused and seeking immediate solutions to complex behaviors. Lunchroom advice and anecdotal approaches may not address the larger needs of students in the classroom. Furthermore, we may be used to approaching students with problem behaviors with a "fix it" mentality, thinking that if we had the correct technique the problem would go away.

Aptner and Propper (1986) suggest that there is no magical "fix-it" answer. We need to think of problem behavior in terms of a troubled system and see the student in a reciprocal context of interaction with the environment. In the systems view, the individual and the environment are both assumed to be active participants reciprocally influencing each other. Aptner and Propper outline a rationale for thinking ecologically. First, past efforts may have failed because the focus may have been too narrow. Second, the child is seldom, if ever, the whole problem. Third, everyone in the child's environment has needs that must be attended to. Fourth, close attention to relationships and linkages may be the single most important determinant of success. Finally, the impact of an ecological approach can go beyond the child.

Bronfenbrenner (1986) talks about various nested systems in which the individual's development takes place. There is the relationship of the person to him or herself. There are one-to-one relationships and interactions among settings in the context of community, work, and school, all of which are set in a particular culture and society. Each one of these relationships influences the individual's development. Frequently, a child's behavior is appropriate in one setting, but seen as entirely inappropriate in another setting. This incongruence is a point of imbalance (Aptner & Propper, 1986). Incongruence, or mismatch, is a disparity between the individual's abilities and the demands or expectations of the environment.

The systems approach sees the child as an inseparable part of a social system. An intervention is the process of helping maintain balance between the individual and the environment in three major areas. First, we look for changes in the child. Second, we change the environment. Third, we change the attitudes and expectations for this individual.

Reflection

Consider your own experience when answering the questions below. Identify various factors that may have influenced your own behaviors while you were growing up.

1. What systems were involved?
2. What kind of support surrounded you?

SYSTEM-WIDE SUPPORT

School-wide structures can support students with learning disabilities and emotional-behavioral disorders. The Individuals with Disabilities Education Act Amendments (1997) require the use of positive behavior support when student behavior interferes with learning. Examining a specific problematic behavior can be helpful, but it is important to examine any behavior in the context of the larger environment. Traditional problem solving has emphasized the examination of the consequences and reinforcers of behavior; positive behavior support tends to learn from all the factors involved in a behavior.

Positive behavior support has several assumptions.

- First, behavior serves a function or a purpose for the individual. Behaviors do not occur "out of the blue" but are meaningful for the individual.

- Second, intervention and behavior support is instructional and preventive. Interventions address antecedent procedures, social skills training, consequence procedures, and especially curricular adaptations.

- Third, interventions are based on individual needs. Needs are assessed across various environments through various means such as formal and informal observations, interviews, and other measures.

- Fourth, interventions are comprehensive and consider long-term outcomes over the span of years. While we try to change behaviors in a short-term context, we do so with long-term outcomes in mind.

Sugai and Carr (1994) have outlined a number of critical components that school staff must consider as system-wide changes. The staff must clearly define expectations and consequences, teach and acknowledge appropriate social behavior. Staff must create a rapid response procedure to dangerous situations and monitor behavior and give feedback.

Students who demonstrate problem behaviors often lack social competence and are simply using the skills with which they negotiate their daily lives. Caught in a well-established coercive cycle, teachers frequently do not recognize that their responses to problem behaviors can actually increase the likelihood that the inappropriate behavior will occur again (Bandura, 1986; Patterson, 1975). Punishment and exclusionary procedures are embedded in school culture (Maag, 2001). Not only do problem behaviors lack congruence within the school environment, but so do the treatments that are intended to address them. Mandating the use of positive behavior support (as in IDEA 97) is an attempt to redress this knowledge gap and discourage the tendency to rely on ineffective and reactive treatment and intervention procedures.

Reflection

Consider your own experience when answering the questions below. Consider a time in your past when a consequence for an inappropriate behavior actually motivated the individual to continue the inappropriate behavior.

1. Describe the circumstances around the event
2. What intervention would you plan to discontinue the inappropriate behavior?

There are life-long implications for individuals who do not achieve basic levels of social competence. In the immediate environment, these students often face academic failure and exclusion from the classroom. This in turn creates a cycle of alienation, reduction of effort, and more failure. Longer-term implications include the risk of terminating participation in school and entering the work force unprepared—a great cost for the individual and society to pay (Blackorby, Edgar, & Kortering, 1991; Rumberger, 1995; Sinclair, Christenson, Evelo, & Hurley, 1998; Wehlage, Rutter, Smith, Lesko, & Fernandez, 1989).

Teachers are at risk as well. When teachers use treatments that are a poor match to the function and purpose of the behavior, the chance of the behavior becoming worse actually increases. If the disruptive behavior continues, reduction of classroom instruction time is the result. Teachers report that this dynamic is common and that they are ill prepared to deal with it. Inability to deal with such challenging behaviors can lead to teacher discouragement and potential burnout. It also models inappropriate adult responses. The unresolved cycles of negative behavior can even lead to the termination of a teaching career (Prater et al., 2000, Weigle, 1997).

Even when a behavior plan is appropriate and a good match, the team faces the challenge of treatment integrity (Gresham, 1989). Are plans implemented as intended? Is there a commitment beyond the initial phase of the treatment (Knoster et al., 2000)? Is a crisis the entry point of the team's plan? Is the treatment acceptable (Fawcett, 1991)?

Positive behavior support is a flexible platform that takes advantage of various models of understanding the child. When trying to understand a child, consider the interactions with a primary caregiver, peer interactions, neighborhood, and even environments that the child never physically enters such as the parent/guardian's workplace (Bronfenbrenner, 1999).

Positive behavior support is a broad range of systematic and individualized strategies for achieving important social and learning outcomes while preventing problem behavior. It is a data-based, proactive, decision-making, and problem-solving process. Positive behavior support emphasizes quality of life in natural settings. A key focus is building responsive environments that systematically favor appropriate student behavior and preferred quality of life outcomes (Bambara, Gomez, Koger, Lohrmann-O'Rourke, & Xin, 2001; Turnbull et al., 2002).

There are three overall components of positive behavior support. The first component, called universal support, considers the largest possible range of the educational environment. Universal support is a school-wide process that requires significant buy-in from stakeholders. Turnbull and associates describe one school community at risk for significant failure. As a first step, this school clearly defined five universal behavioral expectations in simple, succinct, and positive ways. They decided on the following expectations as central for a successful school: be safe, be cooperative, be ready to learn, be respectful, and be responsible. The staff explicitly taught expectations so that all students knew exactly what was expected of them. These values and expectations were extensively communicated on a school-wide basis. For example, teachers and students developed codes of conduct around the five universal expectations—and used lesson plans to teach these values directly in the classroom. A positive reinforcement system was comprehensively implemented. For example, the school developed a ticket system and daily announcement of "winners" with a tangible award, photos, and expectations displayed in the hallway. Finally, by way of a team process, progress was evaluated, making adaptations based on data. For example, teachers asked a series of questions. Has positive interaction increased? Have we experienced a sense of accomplishment? Are students in special education equally included (Turnbull et al., 2002; Weigle, 1997)?

The second component, called group support, consists of delivering intervention to increasingly smaller numbers of students who are experiencing behavioral difficulties. Group support is a means by which administrators and teachers can provide positive behavior support in the largest unit that is feasible for the particular students in need of more intensity. The goal of an assessment is to determine the patterns of appropriate and inappropriate behavior among groups of students. In a local elementary school the teachers noted several environments that needed special attention, such as bathroom areas, doorways during lunch breaks, and hallways before morning classes.

The third component, called individual support, is an intense intervention procedure around an individual student (Turnbull et al., 2002). Individual support is the core intervention that is typically provided to students with disabilities who have problem behaviors. Functional behavioral assessment is a process a team uses to increase treatment effectiveness by matching an intervention with the function of the target behavior. The process promotes hypothesis-driven treatment and places emphasis on skill building (Gable, 1996). It is a process of identifying functional relationships between environmental events and the occurrence or nonoccurrence of a target behavior (Dunlap et al., 1993).

Reflection

Consider your own experience when answering the questions below. Review the material above on positive behavior support.

1. How would a positive behavior support approach assist you to create a smoothly functioning learning community in which students assume responsibility for themselves and one another, participate in decision making, work collaboratively and independently, and engage in purposeful learning activities?
2. Give specific examples of how you might implement positive behavior support in your own classroom.

FUNCTIONAL BEHAVIORAL ASSESSMENT

IDEA 97 requires that a functional behavioral assessment be conducted for a student either before or not later than ten days after a disciplinary action (615.k.1.B.1). Functional behavioral assessment provides a structured procedure to "re-see" not only the student and the behavior of concern, but also the biological, social, affective, and environmental factors that initiate, maintain, or end the behavior in question. Functional behavior assessment helps teachers and families create a collaborative context to examine behaviors. This encourages a focus on problem solving and student growth.

There are four assumptions of functional behavioral assessment:

- every behavior serves a function for the individual.

- behavioral interventions are most effective when they teach the individual what to do instead of what not to do.

- interventions are more effective when they work many people in many places.

- only use a procedure with an individual identified with a disability that you would use with an individual not identified with a disability. (Bambara & Mitchell-Kvacky, 1994).

At the heart of the functional behavioral assessment is the development of a clear picture of the individual in all of his or her different settings. A set of questions forms the steps of the process.

- Who should be on the team?

- What information do we need to make good decisions?

- How will we gather the information?

- What is the target behavior?

- What hypothesis explains the situation?

- What are our measurable goals?

- How can we help the person reach these goals?

- How will we monitor intervention effectiveness?

- Is it working?

- What are the next steps?

Once a team has worked together through a functional behavioral assessment, they begin to view their teaching environment differently. The functional behavioral assessment is rooted in an ecological view of the child. The process influences perspective and assumptions about behavior management.

All of these approaches assume you do not have to go it alone. The teaching profession is changing. Teachers bring higher expectations of collaboration and peer assistance into increasingly complex learning environments. Asking for help and assistance is a sign of wisdom and courage. Team-based and school-wide interventions and behavior support practices are more effective and create environments that support core values of the learning community.

CHAPTER 4: ENGAGING FAMILIES

After completing this section, you will be able to:

- Discuss attending to parents' voices and engaging them in the education of their children
- Identify issues and challenges related to engaging parents and families from various cultural, ethnic, and linguistic groups
- Discuss research on issues specific to various cultures

INTASC PRINCIPLES, KNOWLEDGE, DISPOSITIONS, AND PERFORMANCE

Principle 9: The teacher is a reflective practitioner who continually evaluates the effects of his/her choices and actions on others (students, parents, and other professionals in the learning community) and who actively seeks out opportunities to grow professionally.

Dispositions:
- The teacher is committed to seeking out, developing, and continually refining practices that address the individual needs of students.
- The teacher is committed to reflection, assessment, and learning as an ongoing process.

Principle 10: The teacher fosters relationships with school colleagues, parents, and agencies in the larger community to support students' learning and well-being.

Knowledge:
- The teacher understands how factors in the students' environment outside of school (e.g., family circumstances, community environments, health and economic conditions) may influence students' life and learning.

Performances:
- The teacher establishes respectful and productive relationships with parents and guardians from diverse home and community situations, and seeks to develop cooperative partnerships in support of student learning and well-being.

LISTENING TO AND ENGAGING FAMILIES

Listening to families is an essential part of culturally responsive teaching. Culturally responsive teaching implies that teachers have an ongoing dialog with educators and parents of color in order to understand how school is experienced in different ways (Rethinking Schools, 2000). Teachers and families may have different goals for the education of individual children and may not know much about each others' way of life (Harding, London, & Safer, 2001). Delpit (1995) goes so far as to suggest that parents can be "cultural translators" for teachers and schools.

Harding and associates (1999) argue that the teaching process should begin by finding out about each child's family, particularly about the dreams and expectations the family has for its children.

How schools treat parents and families is more predictive of family engagement than family characteristics. Even when Dauber and Epstein (1993) considered parental education, family size, marital status, socioeconomic level, or student grade level, it was the attitudes and practices of the schools that determined whether or not the families were involved. White-Clark and Decker (1996) contend that many parents judged "hard to reach" are, in fact, self-sufficient, motivated, and involved.

Engagement of parents must be grounded in support rather than change. As a teacher, it isn't your job to "fix" families or "make" them do anything. Rather, it is your role to engage and support them. Dunst, Trivette, & Deal (1988) ground this support in four components. First, they suggest identifying family aspirations and projects that the family considers important enough to devote time and energy to. Second, family strengths and capabilities—those things the family already does well—should be emphasized. Third, when working individually with families, the personal and social network should be mapped to identify both existing sources of support and untapped resources. Finally, the family should be empowered to become more competent in mobilizing resources to meet its needs and achieve desired goals.

Reflection

Consider your own experience when answering the questions below. Frame your response in terms of the four components of support described by Dunst, Trivette, and Deal (1988).

1. Were parents welcomed at your school?
2. What sorts of activities, procedures, or attitudes promoted that welcome?
3. What were things that made parents feel unwelcome?

ISSUES AND CHALLENGES IN ENGAGING FAMILIES

One of the key challenges in engaging families from various ethnic, cultural, or linguistic groups is to learn about the culture while avoiding making meaningless generalizations. For example, in their study of Latino parents of students in special education, Bailey and associates (1999) reported the family heritage varied widely. Families differed in the awareness of, use of, and satisfaction with school and services. General beliefs about family characteristics and student outcomes did not seem to be related.

Because of these challenges, Harry, Rueda, and Kalyanpur (1999) suggest that teachers recognize their own cultural values. Teachers need to assume a posture of "cultural reciprocity" (p. 125). In cultural reciprocity, teachers examine what they teach and how they teach for the cultural grounding of the content and process rather than assuming that curriculum and methods stem from universal values. For example, teachers cannot assume that every parent would want his or her child to stand up for him or herself in class, working independently and competitively. Parents from various cultures may prefer that their children support the group, work collaboratively, and assume a respectful silence rather than speaking out. Understanding the belief systems behind your teaching is a way to begin seeing what may be challenging to parents of various cultures. In the Video Case featuring Guy Jones, he provides the example of the Thanksgiving Story and how it may be offensive to Native American children.

In addition to examining assumptions about what and how to teach, teachers need to be careful to avoid assumptions about parents and their role in their child's education. Chavkin and Williams (1993) found that African American and Latino families expressed the desire to be more involved with their children's education, help with homework, and have more influence on what happens in school. Ninety-seven percent said that they worked at cooperating with their children's teachers. Parents demonstrated their interest in their children's education by attending school performances, helping their children with their homework, and lending a hand at school events.

In working with families from various cultural groups, teachers should be aware of power relations. Delpit (1995) describes the strand of power in education. Compulsory education is a system's power over the individual. The school system has the power to determine another's intelligence or normalcy. Teachers have power over students. Education itself has power over economic status. For those from privileged cultures, education is an assumption, and the power granted institutions and individuals is not viewed as hampering, but rather as helping.

RESEARCH ABOUT ENGAGING FAMILIES FROM VARIOUS CULTURAL GROUPS

The concepts of race and ethnicity are often confused. Hodgkinson (2001) further explains that the 2000 census made these issues even more complex. The 2000 census allowed the individual completing the form to check as many race boxes as he or she chose. Three thousand black Hispanics in the United States checked "black" on the census form because they do not consider "Hispanic" a race. At least 40 percent of all Americans have had some racial mixing in the last three generations, but only 2 to 4 percent reported it on Census 2000.

Hodgkinson (2001) contends that it is more useful for teachers to consider "national origin" than race. He uses the example of knowing that a student is Hispanic, which gives you little information, versus knowing that a student is Cuban or Mexican. In terms of national origin or culture, he suggests that there are three major differences in how various peoples see the world. First, in terms of time, Americans generally believe in the future. However, many cultures have a strong sense of the past and "now." Arguing that students need to learn in order to be ready for the future may not, with some cultures, be as helpful as suggesting that it will help them connect with the past. Second, in terms of family, most Americans think of the nuclear or immediate family, whereas many other cultures have large extended families and strong ties of kinship. Finally, Americans typically have little sense of hierarchy. Many cultures, however, have rigid structures with specific ideas about the place of children and women.

We began this discussion by suggesting that generalizations about members of a specific ethnic, cultural, or linguistic group are dangerous. As Guild (1994) argues, "generalizations about a group of people have often led to naïve inferences about individuals within that group" (p. 16). Keep this in mind as we discuss the findings of research related to the four largest cultural groups in U.S. schools.

African American families
The deficit view of African American families continues to have an impact on teachers' interactions with parents (Harry, 1992). Teachers often relegate African American families, based on assumptions about their knowledge and interest in participation, to the role of "consent-giver" rather than full participant. In addition, assumptions about discipline in African American homes are often made. Nweke (1994) reported that although African American parents and Anglo parents punish the same misbehavior of their children, the time and place of the punishment differs. African American families may address behaviors in public that Anglo parents address in private. In addition, in African American families, almost 90 percent reported that the mother was responsible for discipline, whereas in Anglo families only about 50 percent said mothers were responsible for discipline.

Boykin and Bailey's (2000) work about culturally relevant factors, also discussed in the first section of this booklet, was grounded in the home socialization experiences, values, practices, and preferences of African American students from low-income backgrounds. Attitudes and practices in these homes tended to be communal, intense, lively, and variable. Family members worked together in groups rather than individually. Music and movement were an important part of family life. In addition, there was a high energy level in the homes.

Latino families
In Latino homes, children are usually nurtured by a large number of relatives. Inger (1992), however, suggests that these families often do not extend their interaction to the schools, and the reserve and non-confrontational manner of Latino parents may be misinterpreted as lack of interest in their child's education. Because of the emphasis on the family, Latino families may be reluctant to send their children to preschool (Lewis, 1993), and though the care of the children is shared by large numbers of relatives, parents are hesitant to extend this care giving to schools (Nicolau & Ramos, 1990). The issue of language also emerges in working with Latino families.

Asian American families

A large number of ethnic, cultural, and linguistic groups are referred to as Asian American families. The largest of these subgroups are Pacific islanders, southeast Asians, and east Asians. These cultures vary within, as well as among, each group. For example, simply knowing that one of your students is Vietnamese doesn't provide enough information—he or she may be from a Christian, French-educated family, or may be Hmong, a culture with no written language (Schwartz, 1994).

Typically, Asian parents view teachers as the professionals who have authority over the child's schooling. Parents, then, shouldn't interfere, and a teacher who asks for help may be viewed as incompetent. Communication in Asian culture often relies on shared assumptions, nonverbal signals, and courtesy. Teachers may misinterpret these beliefs and behaviors as parents being apathetic about their child's education or being submissive during conversations.

Native American families

Native American families have experienced significant challenges to their identity, including having children removed from the family for compulsory boarding school and foster placement, high drop-out rates, over-identification as special education students, high rates of alcohol and drug abuse, high suicide rates, chronic health problems, and low income (Grimm, 1992). There may be great mistrust of schools, in that formal education has been used as a vehicle for assimilating and detribalizing members of Indian nations (Joe & Malach, 1998). Ceremonial life may be confidential or private, and questions regarding practice are inappropriate. As with all families, beginning with cross cultural themes—children, home, families, community, and the environment—young children can learn about native peoples rather than cultural stereotypes (Jones & Moomaw, 2002).

Reflection

Consider your own experience when answering the questions below. There is great variation among the members of any cultural group.

1. Is it worthwhile to discuss cultural characteristics?
2. Do the differences outweigh the similarities?
3. When does a discussion of cultural characteristics become a discussion of stereotypes?

WORKING WITH "OTHER PEOPLE'S CHILDREN"

So what does a teacher who is committed to working with families and communities do in his or her classroom? At the risk of presenting a laundry list or cookbook, teachers can engage in some specific activities or behaviors.

Be flexibile

Teachers should develop a flexible and self-directed teaching approach to working with families and students rooted in the use of natural language. Corson (1998) suggests that this includes a readiness to meet unusual classroom events or situations in imaginative and creative ways. This flexibility must be grounded in a person-oriented approach to conflict resolution that is sensitive to the different values and norms of various students.

Examine curriculum

Your curriculum should build critical thinkers who can make decisions about their lives, address societal and social problems, and ask how change can occur (Corson, 1998). Multicultural activities should be integrated fully into the school curriculum, rather than being restricted to one-shot or culture-of-the-month sessions (Cotton, 1995).

Engage in ongoing professional development

Culturally responsive teachers are professionally active in learning about diversity. They are willing to look at how the school, not the student, is contributing to educational failure (Corson, 1998). They are continually learning about culture, class, gender, race, sexual orientation, religion, and other phenomena that affect or reflect the human context in which their students are developing (Harding, London, & Safer, 2001). They must realize that fighting racism is not primarily the job of people of color, and continue to examine their practices that perpetuate the system of power and privilege (Weiss, 2002).

Go beyond simple labels

Knowing that a student is identified as "Hispanic" gives you very little information. The family's country of origin, the language the family uses at home, and parents' proficiency at English should be explored if you are to meet the needs of the student (Hodgkinson, 2001). Students who are identified as white are actually white ethnic students—Italian Americans, Irish Americans, Jewish Americans, Polish Americans, Appalachians, etc. —all of whom have unique customs, holidays, practices, and family interactions (Ladson-Billings, 2001).

Be aware of your own culture

Ladson-Billings (2001) suggests that white, middle-class prospective teachers have little or no understanding of their own culture because notions of whiteness are taken for granted. However, white ethnic students may refer to themselves as Italian or Irish or Polish because their socio-economic status makes it difficult for them to identify with whiteness. Though few Americans have one heritage or identity, the traditions we observe are unique, and part of who we are. Understanding your personal history and family "stories" is important in your understanding of the stories of other people's children.

Recognize parents' racial consciousness

In Xu's (2001) study of families of children in an urban middle school, parents were aware of their own racial and ethnic identities. Parents expressed an awareness of their family racial identities and the desire that their children be taught how to get along with people from other races. The parents' racial consciousness was exacerbated by the fact that the staff was predominately white. Parents expressed concerns that white teachers wanted African American parents to deal with behaviors "their way" rather than the way the family traditionally dealt with misbehavior. In their conversations they frequently referred to teachers as "they" and children of color as "our kids."

PART II: CULTURALLY RESPONSIVE TEACHING IN ACTION

CASE 1: SECOND GRADE LITERACY IN AN URBAN SCHOOL

Educators want children to achieve. However, with intense efforts to increase the performance of young children in urban areas, direct skill instruction may emerge as the primary emphasis. Well-meaning individuals sometimes make statements about what "those students" need. Yet teachers in urban schools work hard to develop a climate in which every child is challenged, feels safe, and experiences the joy of learning. In this classroom you will observe Janice Glaspie and Darwin Henderson working with Ms. Glaspie's second graders, using literature to enhance their literacy learning. After viewing the case, see if you agree with Ms. Glaspie's statement "my children are literate."

Addressing stereotyping
One of the most important considerations when presenting literature representing various cultures is to insure that the literature does not present stereotypes. Stereotypes may result in inaccurate, inappropriate, and harmful generalizations (Hanson, 1998). Information about various cultures should be used as a basis for respectful interaction rather than to characterize all members of a cultural group.

Understanding historical contexts
When working with children from diverse ethnic, cultural, or linguistic groups, the stories in their textbooks may not reflect their history. Willis (1998) contends that much of the history is only now being told. He suggests that the history of various groups is essential in that the path to freedom and equality has shaped the lives of the original members of the group and their descendants just as their cultural heritage and accomplishments have helped shape the nation.

Respectful language
The language used in a classroom must reflect the way in which the teacher and students value each other's contributions. In view of discussing various groups, Anglesey (1997) maintains that a people should be able to say what is respectful and what isn't.

Contributions of men and women
Both genders should be represented both in the professionals who work with students and in the materials presented in them. Equal recognition of men and women has resulted in reexamination and redefinition of equal access (Hanson, 1998) in both academics and extracurricular opportunities.

Selection of materials
The first consideration in selecting ethnic materials is that they must be good literature (Tompkins, 2003). In addition, the materials should be rich in cultural details, use

authentic dialogue, and present cultural issues in enough depth that readers can think and talk about them. The inclusion of cultural group members should be purposeful, not just to fill a quota.

Engaging students

Students must be engaged in order to learn. Grant and Sleeter (1998) suggest that in some cases the teacher may need to build "bridges to the curriculum" to enable students to succeed and to adapt to the requirements of the traditional classroom.

Culturally sensitive illustration

Culturally sensitive illustrations can increase the students' opportunities to identify with the literature (Tompkins, 2003). The illustrations should be of high quality and may help challenge students' assumptions about various cultures.

Discussion Questions

1. One teaching behavior used extensively in this classroom is wait time. What are some of the implications of the silences in the room?

2. Ms. Glaspie is explicit about helping her students become literate and being able to discuss literature. What is some of the language she models that is then used by her students?

Questions for Consideration

1. Both of the professionals in this classroom and all of the students are African American. Is this a "diverse" setting? What are some of the meanings of the term "diversity"?

2. Many individuals recommend controlled reading materials and direct instruction in basic skills for children attending schools such as the one included in this case. What would this classroom look like if that was the approach used? How would it be the same? How would it be different?

CASE 2: THE EMERGING COMPETENCE OF YOUTH—
A MIDDLE SCHOOL CLASSROOM

As students grow into early adolescence, they experience an increasing desire for independence and opportunities to demonstrate competence and mastery. Mastery of materials and one's self requires a careful balance of a safe environment with an environment that empowers the individual with choice and decision making opportunities. In this science classroom, Cathy Burton works with students to make connections to other content areas as well as to worldwide issues that face us, using poster projects and presentations on diseases. After viewing the case, brainstorm some ideas about how educators can balance the complex needs of students at various stages of their human development.

Models affirmation
All humans need encouragement to take risks in the learning environment. Teachers grow in the art of encouragement and affirmation. Freedman (1993) refers to the art of mentoring as having critical components that include: (1) listening to youth, (2) being "youth driven," (3) building a relationship, (4) respecting boundaries, (5) being sensitive to differences, (6) focusing on youth, (7) providing support and challenge, (8) acknowledging reciprocity, (9) being realistic, and (10) duration over time.

Capitalizes on students' cultural backgrounds
Educators have to think through the learning experience of the student in order to make solid and explicit connection to the daily lives of the learners. Resnick (1987) suggests that school learning is often discontinuous with daily life of learners from various economic, ethnic, cultural, and language groups. In schools, individual rather than group cognition is valued; schools emphasize mental activity rather than using tools; symbols are manipulated rather than contextual reasoning.

Becomes authentic and child centered
Education is not something that teachers do to children. A relationship is implied. Learning is reciprocal and takes place in both directions. Bronfenbrenner (1999) suggests that for development to occur, the person must engage in an activity. To be effective, the activity must take place on a regular basis, over an extended period. An occasional weekend of doing things with one's mom or dad does not count, nor do activities that are often interrupted. This is because, to be developmentally effective, activities must take place long enough to become "increasingly more complex." Mere repetition does not work. Developmentally effective proximal processes are not unidirectional; there must be initiation and response in both directions. Proximal processes are not limited to interpersonal interaction; they can also involve interaction with objects and symbols. Under these circumstances, for reciprocal interaction to occur, the objects and symbols in the immediate environment must invite attention, exploration, manipulation, elaboration, and imagination.

Addresses various learning styles
Nothing happens in isolation. Educators are aware of the total environment and the values that drive the educational process. For example, Sapon-Shevin (1994) explains that cooperative learning begs that we pay attention to the norms of student empowerment throughout the day. If

teachers do not feel empowered, they will not be able to empower children. When competition, tracking, and exclusion are widespread, the culture of the school sends a different message. Without a critical approach to how school culture is structured, the inherent contradictions may create significant inhibitors.

Thinks critically

Power relations are implicit in the educational process. Teachers are aware that much more is at stake than the immediate content of the lesson being taught at any one moment in time. Delpit (1995) suggests that it is vital to give voice to alternative worldviews. This involves incorporating a range of pedagogical orientations. Teachers must be aware of power relations. Examples include compulsory education as a system's power over the individual, the power of a teacher over a student, the power to determine another's intelligence or normalcy, and the power of an education to prepare for a particular type of job.

Emphasizes belonging to a learning community

Brendtro and Brokenleg (2001) contend that the goal of discipline is to teach courage, not submission. The use of coercive discipline and harsh corporal punishment are manifestations of the mindset of the Western mentality of child rearing. "You are acting like a child," is a phrase that is interpreted as an insult in Western culture. Belonging is the organizing principle in Indian cultures. Significance is assured by belonging, whereas in Western cultural values, one gains significance by standing out from the others.

Connects to students' homes and cultures

Making connections to the families of the students in our classrooms is an aspect of the systems approach to learning. Dunst et al. (1988) provides a four-component model to support families: (1) identify family aspirations and projects that the family considers important enough to devote time and energy to; (2) identify family strengths and capabilities to emphasize the things the family already does well to help mobilize resources to meet needs; (3) map the family's personal and social network to identify both existing sources of support and resources untapped but potential sources of aid and assistance; and (4) function in a number of different roles to enable and empower the family to become more competent in mobilizing resources to meet its needs and achieve desired goals.

Discussion Questions

1. Ms. Burton, in a mini-lesson at the beginning of class, assists students in the process of making connections to other class content as well as worldwide concerns. What style or approach does this educator use to encourage student participation?

2. Students in this classroom make presentations on sensitive issues concerning, for example, sexuality. Yet we do not see or hear signs of nervousness or discomfort. What aspects of school climate need to be fostered in order to create a safe environment where issues of vulnerability are addressed?

Questions for Consideration

1. The content and presentation in this case is taking place near the end of the school year. Could these presentations have taken place at the beginning of the year?

2. A teacher-centered classroom might present the content of this unit in a very different way. What values do you think guide this educator's classroom planning? Which values do you identify with? What values might guide you to plan differently?

CASE 3: ONE TEACHER'S INFLUENCE?

In this case, you listened to a teacher, Ms. Joy Lohrer, who saw something happening in the school concerning diversity. She responded to the need. Rather than impose some structure, she turned to the students for ideas and dreams. Ms. Lohrer initially provided the specific agenda of the tolerance training videos and from there generated a list of student-desired activities. This educator made a commitment to meet each Thursday. Her goal was to listen to students.

Sometimes schools deal with things by not dealing with them. Not sure of what other educators were doing in their classrooms, this educator noted little or no attention to current events or diversity concerns in the public sphere of the building. Teachers may feel constrained. The school may inadvertently blind itself to outside world events. School staff may find itself in crisis without a framework within which to respond. When all teachers can think of is enacting more discipline and getting the consequences more consistent, the staff may need to take a few steps back to reflect critically on their vision. From the first day of class, educators and students need to be reminded that diversity and equity are part of the mission.

Identifying the problem using critical thinking
Ethnic labels can act in positive and negative ways. Who names whom? Heath & McLaughlin (1993) suggest that ethnicity may be a subjective view a group holds regarding its common membership because of shared descent or historical background and similarities of customs, language, and sometimes physical type. However, those enclosed within those views may not acknowledge linguistic and cultural features that mark boundaries from the perspective of outsiders. Certain groups can label other groups as "ethnic groups."

Getting a clear picture of the culture and its impact on education
When we first enter, an environment may offer many forms of information. Clothing styles and use of language carry codes that we may not understand. Even if we have awareness, we may be unclear about the meaning of the information we are receiving. Clifford Geertz, in his *Interpretation of Cultures* (1973), talks about the various levels of description of reality. Only a native makes first order interpretations of his or her own culture. Second order interpretations come from those outside the culture. It is one thing to bring home a mask from another culture and have no idea what the artifact means, and quite another to reduce the "puzzlement." by way of interpretation. An interpretation is an attempt to reduce the puzzlement. Geertz (1973) contends that we are suspended in webs of significance.

Equitable and just structures and environments
Educators facilitate learning on multiple levels. We may need to learn technical aspects of math, but we also learn about how math skills can open doors in our lives beyond the schoolhouse. Gay (2000) suggests that culturally responsive teachers use the cultural knowledge, experiences, and learning styles of students to make learning more appropriate and effective for them. Sleeter (2000) suggests that the central issue is one of justice.

Context of educational opportunities—caring

The world we live in is complex and changing. So too are our students. Coots et al. (1995) compares school organization in the past to a factory system, each grade a new place on the assembly line, to provide an education to the masses. In the interests of efficiency students who could not "keep up" or who required additional assistance were placed in separate programs. A new educational system requires collaboration and attention to flexibility and differentiated learning so that everyone receives the support necessary to develop.

Instructional strategies (practical rationality)

Learning styles differ according to culture, region, community, and gender, to name a few. Gollnick (2002) indicates that gender differentiation is a dynamic we pay attention to. For example, girls are more likely to learn in cooperative mathematics activities, and are influenced positively by teacher praise of a correct answer. Boys achieve better when the teacher corrects a wrong answer. Awareness of various strategies and attentiveness to preferred learning styles (Gardner et al., 1986) is an essential teaching strategy in a gender-sensitive curriculum.

Empowering the student

Cultural competence begins with a growing knowledge of where we are each located and formed by forces in our own cultural experiences. Harry et al. (1999) suggests that many professionals have turned to the majority culture for guidelines regarding what is culturally normative and culturally valued. We must have a commitment to cultural reciprocity. Understanding one's own cultural values becomes a point of reference from which to understand differing perspectives. We must cultivate the habit of examining the cultural underpinnings of the specific beliefs from which our service ideals arise.

Accommodations and adaptations

In one classroom, students express diversity in terms of background knowledge, readiness and language, preferences in learning, interests, and responsiveness. The goal of a differentiated learning procedure would be to maximize each student's growth and individual success. The process assesses learners where they are and builds instruction from there. Content, process, and products are three key elements of differentiation (Tomlinson, 2001).

Discussion Questions

1. Ms. Lohrer has seen a need in her building and begun to collaborate with students to address their concerns. What are the signs and kinds of messages that a teacher would look for in a school environment to determine if there is a need that requires a supportive response?

2. Teachers need to know how to help people work productively and cooperatively in complex social environments. Imagine feeling isolated in your teaching context. Are there things you can do to break that isolation or do you just form a stiff upper lip and get through the day? What would be your first steps?

Questions for Consideration

1. What are your points of connection to relate to and understand others? What really matters to students when they consider who their teachers are?

2. Unfortunately, teachers feeling isolated is not as uncommon as we would like it to be. What characteristics of the teaching profession might help create such isolation? What characteristics in our profession might lead us away from isolation?

CASE 4: CHALLENGING CULTURAL ASSUMPTIONS

Our culture is an integral part of our development and the assumptions we make about others and ourselves. In this case, Guy Jones, Hunkpapa Lakota and a full-blood member of the Standing Rock Sioux Nation, discusses assumptions that may have an impact on the self-concept of young children. In this conversation with his colleague Sally Moomaw, various classroom practices in classrooms, some of which are imbedded in our own experiences as students and teachers, are laid bare in view of another culture.

Forced assimilation
Forced assimilation attempts to make the traditional parts of the students' life invisible. This is a challenge to the child's identity, and in direct conflict with Abda-Haqq's (1994) indication that culturally responsive curriculum capitalizes on students' cultural backgrounds rather than attempting to override or negate them.

Challenges to self-concept
Efforts to assimilate members of a cultural group can be a challenge to the individual's self-concept. Spindler and Spindler (1994) describe five responses: (a) reaffirmation of culture; (b) constructive marginality in which personal culture is usually constructed of several different segments, some of which are Euro-American; (c) withdrawal because of the inability to remain traditional and yet not being able to fit into the white world; (d) biculturalism, moving between the traditional and Euro-American culture; and (e) assimilation, forced conforming to Euro-American culture.

Dealing with stereotypes
Sometimes our efforts to learn about cultures in itself supports stereotypes. Lynch (1998) contends that assuming that culture-specific information gathered from books or "diversity training" applies to all individuals from the cultural group is not only inaccurate but also dangerous and leads to stereotyping. The goal, in her view, should be insight, not stereotype.

Impact of genocide on culture
The potential for alienation among groups against whom there has been an elimination and assimilation effort is obviously significant (LaFramboise and Low, 1989).

Teacher rigidity and assumptions
Teacher rigidity can literally silence students. An example is the requirement that students speak English outside of the classroom. Traditional languages are an essential element of life, culture, and identity. Formal schooling can no longer be seen as a vehicle for assimilating and detribalizing (Joe & Malach, 1998).

Rights of people to respectful communication

One of the key issues in working with people from diverse ethnic and cultural groups is that of respectful communication. Anglesey (1997) suggests that this begins with recognizing that each people has a right to name itself, define its own history, and live according to its own culture.

Suggestions for teachers

One of the most important things a teacher can do is be aware that until very recently education efforts directed at Indians were based on the assumption that Indian people are inferior to white people (Harjo, 1999). Similar to the issues of women and other cultures, history books relegate Indian matters to a few pages or comments. The history of the people is usually treated with ignorance, misrepresentation, and apathy.

Discussion Questions

1. What are some of the challenges to self-concept that can occur every day in a classroom?

2. List some of the symbols related to Native Americans that may continue the stereotypes

Questions for Consideration

1. The use of mascots representing Native Americans is entrenched in our culture. Are these indeed offensive? Do native peoples have a valid complaint about their use?

2. Guy Jones does not have an issue with being called an Indian, and refers to himself as such. Does the naming of a cultural group matter? Who should determine the "politically correct" phrase to use for a people?

PART III: RESOURCES

PERFORMANCE ASSESSMENT ACTIVITIES

Each of the following performance assessment activities provides evidence for the indicated Principles of the Interstate New Teacher Assessment and Support Consortium (INTASC). We hope responding to these probes will assist you, the student, in constructing knowledge of culturally responsive instruction.

Before beginning each activity, refer to the Rubric Assessment. This rubric will help you compose a paper illustrating your understanding of the specific CEC Standard being addressed. Demonstrating your understanding of the concept by providing related literature references through numerous examples and an integrated analysis, your professor will be able to determine your understanding of the specific standard. Your professor will evaluate your paper according to the following scale:

    1—You have an unacceptable knowledge;
    2—You have a basic knowledge;
    3—You have a proficient knowledge; or
    4—You have an outstanding knowledge of the standard

INTASC Principle 3: The teacher understands how students differ in their approaches to learning and creates instructional opportunities that are adapted to diverse learners.

Knowledge:
- The teacher understands and can identify differences in approaches to learning and performance, including different learning styles, multiple intelligences, and performance modes, and can design instruction that helps use students' strengths as the basis for growth.
- The teacher has a well-grounded framework for understanding cultural and community diversity and knows how to learn about and incorporate students' experiences, cultures, and community resources into instruction.

Task: Generate a narrative one to two pages in length which:
- describes culturally responsive instruction
- provides specific examples from one or more cases which provide examples of culturally responsive instruction

Rubric for Assessment

Rating → Content ↓	Unacceptable 1	Basic 2	Proficient 3	Outstanding 4
Defines concept	Inaccurate or missing definition	Superficial understanding; copies words from text	Demonstrates understanding of the concept	Demonstrates understanding of the concept and provides related literature
Exemplars	Missing or misidentified examples	One or two obvious examples	Three or more examples analyzed and contrasted	Four or more examples analyzed and contrasted
Clarity and organization	Rambling; single paragraph; grammatical/spelling errors	Simple essay format	Essay format, clear advance organizer and summary	Integrated analysis

INTASC Principle 5: The teacher uses an understanding of individual and group motivation and behavior to create a learning environment that encourages positive social interaction, active engagement in learning, and self-motivation.

Task: Choose one of the two classroom cases. Analyze the instructional strategies used by the teacher and the ways in which these strategies also support the classroom climate.

Rubric for Assessment

Rating ➜ Content ⬇	Unacceptable 1	Basic 2	Proficient 3	Outstanding 4
Provides context for narrative	Not provided	Simple context provided	Multilevel description of context	Detailed description of context
Exemplars	Missing or misidentified examples	One or two obvious examples	Three or more examples analyzed and contrasted	Four or more examples analyzed and contrasted
Clarity and organization	Rambling; single paragraph; grammatical/spelling errors	Simple essay format	Essay format, clear advance organizer and summary	Integrated analysis
Analysis	No analysis; lists	Simple analysis	Analyzes and contrasts learning strategies and climate	Detailed analysis and integration of description of strategies and climate

INTASC Principle 3: The teacher understands how students differ in their approaches to learning and creates instructional opportunities that are adapted to diverse learners

Knowledge:
- The teacher understands and can identify differences in approaches to learning and performance, including different learning styles, multiple intelligences, and performance modes, and can design instruction that helps use students' strengths as the basis for growth
- The teacher has a well-grounded framework for understanding cultural and community diversity and knows how to learn about and incorporate students' experiences, cultures, and community resources into instruction

Task: Review the two classroom cases. Generate a chart in which you provide exemplars of each of these general considerations of culturally responsive instruction:
- utilizing cultural themes in instruction.
- utilizing cooperative learning.
- recognizing a vision of quality schooling for all students.

Rating➜ Content⬇	Unacceptable 1	Basic 2	Proficient 3	Outstanding 4
Format	Not presented as chart	Presented as chart; single examples only	Presented in chart; more than one example in several areas	Presented in chart; several examples in each area
Accuracy	Several missing items or inaccurately identified items	Few inaccurately identified items	No inaccurately identified items	Items accurately identified and explained
Presentation	Confusing; unclear	Clear communication, few grammatical errors	No grammatical errors; clear communication	Compelling arguments; no errors

INTASC Principle 4: The teacher understands and uses a variety of instructional strategies to encourage students' development of critical thinking, problem solving, and performance skills.

Dispositions: The teacher values flexibility and reciprocity in the teaching process as necessary for adapting instruction to student responses, ideas, and needs.

Task: There are three elements of differentiated instruction: content, process, and product (Tomlinson, 2001). Review either the Second Grade or Middle School class. Identify various ways in which content, process, or product are differentiated for the students who vary from their peers. Using your own experience, describe a hypothetical lesson and the ways in which you would adjust content, process, or product. This should be completed in a written narrative.

Rating➡ Content⬇	Unacceptable 1	Basic 2	Proficient 3	Outstanding 4
Clarity and accuracy of presentation	Unclear; inaccurate; rambling	Presentation is understandable; contains few errors	Presentation easy to understand; no errors	Well-written, articulate presentation
Indicators	Missing indicator(s)	One simple example or counter-example	Two or three examples or counter-examples; explanation	Several indicators; complex discussion
Presentation	Confusing; unclear	Clear communication, few grammatical errors	No grammatical errors; clear communication	Compelling arguments; no errors
Accuracy	Several missing items or inaccurately identified items	Few inaccurately identified items	No inaccurately identified items	Items accurately identified and explained
Summarization and reflection	No summarization or reflection	Simple summarization	Summarization and reflection	Insightful summarization and reflection

INTASC Principle 3: The teacher understands how students differ in their approaches to learning and creates instructional opportunities that are adapted to diverse learners.

Knowledge:
- The teacher understands and can identify differences in approaches to learning and performance, including different learning styles, multiple intelligences, and performance modes, and can design instruction that helps use students' strengths as the basis for growth.
- The teacher has a well-grounded framework for understanding cultural and community diversity and knows how to learn about and incorporate students' experiences, cultures, and community resources into instruction.

Task: Boykin (1994, 1988) identified nine interrelated but distinct dimensions manifest in terms of stylistic behaviors in the lives of African Americans. They include:

- spirituality—a vitalistic rather than mechanistic approach to life.

- harmony—the belief that humans and nature are harmoniously conjoined.

- movement expressiveness—an emphasis on the interweaving of movement, rhythm, percussiveness, music, and dance.

- verve—the special receptiveness to relatively high levels of sensate stimulation.

- affect—an emphasis on emotion and feelings.

- communication—a commitment to social connectedness where social bonds transcend individual privileges.

- expressive individualism—the cultivation of distinctive personality and a proclivity for spontaneity in behavior.

- orality—a preference for oral/aural modalities of communication.

- social time perspective—an orientation in which time is treated as passing through a social space rather than a material one.

Review the video case of Janice's second grade classroom. What aspects of these dimensions are present in the classroom? Discuss each of the dimensions that are present and provide an example. Present your findings in a chart.

Rating➜ Content⬇	Unacceptable 1	Basic 2	Proficient 3	Outstanding 4
Format	Not presented as chart	Presented as chart; single examples only	Presented in chart; more than one example in several areas	Presented in chart; several examples in each area
Accuracy	Several missing items or inaccurately identified items	Few inaccurately identified items	No inaccurately identified items	Items accurately identified and explained
Presentation	Confusing; unclear	Clear communication, few grammatical errors	No grammatical errors; clear communication	Compelling arguments; no errors

SAMPLE RESPONSES TO CASE DISCUSSION QUESTIONS

Case 1: Second Grade Literacy in an Urban School

1. One teaching behavior used extensively in this classroom is wait time. What are some of the implications of the silences in the room?

   - Students are provided time to visually examine
   - Students are given adequate time to reply
   - Students with communication challenges contribute
   - The classroom tone is reflective rather than reactive

2. Ms. Glaspie is explicit about helping her students become literate and being able to discuss literature. What is some of the language she models that is then used by her students?

   - Illustrator
   - Author
   - Literature circles
   - Theme
   - Character
   - Setting

Case 2: The Emerging Competence of Youth—A Middle School Classroom

1. Ms. Burton, in a mini-lesson at the beginning of class, assists students in the process of making connections to other class content as well as worldwide concerns. What style or approach does this educator use to encourage student participation?

   - Wait time
   - Open ended questions
   - Suggesting wider topics of consideration
   - Affirming all responses given

2. Students in this classroom make presentations on sensitive issues, for example, concerning sexuality. Yet we do not see or hear signs of nervousness or discomfort. What aspects of school climate need to be fostered in order to create a safe environment where issues of vulnerability are addressed?

   - Modeling listening skills
   - Class discussion about what makes learners nervous or uncomfortable
   - How to move beyond comfort zones
   - Specific teaching of tolerance
   - Open conversations that occur on a regular basis to build expectations

Case 3: One Teacher's Influence

1. Ms. Lohrer has seen a need in her building and begun to collaborate with students to address their concerns. What are the signs and kinds of messages that a teacher would look for in a school environment to determine if there is a need that requires a supportive response?

   - Student complaints
   - Pattern behaviors that occur in spite of consequences
   - Topics that students regularly initiate for discussion
   - Student requests for activities and attention

2. Teachers need to know how to help people work productively and cooperatively in complex social environments. Imagine feeling isolated in your teaching context. Are there things you can do to break that isolation or do you just form a stiff upper lip and get through the day? What would be your first steps?

   - Create a short interest survey for a faculty meeting
   - Lunch room conversation topics
   - Learn about past efforts at various activities
   - Locate a couple of support teachers and specifically request their assistance

Case 4: Challenging Cultural Assumptions

1. What are some of the challenges to self-concept that can occur every day in a classroom?

   - Being singled out
   - Assumptions grounded in stereotypes
   - Assumptions related to ideas of homogeneity of members of the cultural group
   - Generally accepted symbols
   - Assumptions about life style

2. List some of the symbols related to Native Americans that may continue the stereotypes.

   - Sports mascots
   - Thanksgiving stories

REFERENCES

Abda-Haqq, I. (1994). *Culturally responsive curriculum*. ERIC Digest (ERIC Document Services ED370936). Washington, DC: ERIC Clearinghouse on Teaching and Teacher Education.

Anglesey, Z. (1997). Moving from an obsolete lingo to a vocabulary of respect. *Multicultural Review, 6*(3), 23-28.

Aptner, S. J., & Propper, C. A. (1986). Ecological perspectives on youth violence. In S. J. Aptner & A. P. Goldstein (Eds.), *Youth violence: Programs and prospects* (pp. 140-159). New York: Pergamon.

Bailey, D. B., Jr., Skinner, D., Correa, V., Arcia, E., Reyes, Blanes, M. E., Rodriguez, P., Vazquez-Montilla, E., & Skinner, M. (1999). Needs and supports reported by Latino families of young children with developmental disabilities. *Journal on Mental Retardation, 104*(5), 437-445.

Bambara, L. M., Gomez, O., Koger, F., Lohrmann-O'Rourke, S., & Xin, Y. P. (2001). More than techniques: Team members' perspectives on implementing positive supports for adults with severe challenging behaviors. *Journal of the Association for Persons with Severe Handicaps, 26*(4), 213-228.

Bambara, L. M., & Mitchell-Kvacky, N. A. (1994). Positive behavior support for students with severe disabilities: An emerging multicomponent approach for addressing challenging behaviors. *School Psychology Review, 23*(2), 263-278.

Bandura, A. (1986). *Social foundations of thought and action: A social cognitive theory*. Englewood Cliffs, NJ: Prentice Hall.

Bennett, C. (2001). Genres of research in multicultural education. *Review of Educational Research, 71*(2), 171-217.

Bennis, W. G. & Nanus, B. (1985). *Leaders: The strategies for taking charge*. New York: Harper Collins.

Bizzell, P. (1994). "Contact zones" and English studies. *College English, 52*(2), 163-169.

Blackorby, J., Edgar, E., & Kortering, L. J. (1991). A third of our youth? A look at the problem of high school dropout among students with mild handicaps. *The Journal of Special Education, 25*(1), 102-113.

Boykin, A. W. (1994). Afrocultural expression and its implications for schooling. In E. R. Hollins, J. E. King, & W. C. Hayman (Eds.), Teaching diverse populations: Formulating a knowledge base (pp. 243-256). Albany, NY: SUNY Press.

Boykin, A. W., & Allen, B. A. (1988). Rhythmic movement facilitated learning in working-class Afro-American children. *Journal of Genetic Psychology, 149*(3), 335-347.

Boykin, C. T. & Bailey, C. J. (2000). *The role of cultural factors in school relevant cognitive functioning: Description of home environmental factors, cultural orientations, and learning preferences*. Washington, DC: Center for Research on the Education of Students at Risk.

Brendtro, L., & Brokenleg, M. (2001). The circle of courage: Children as sacred beings. In L. Lantieri (Ed.), *Schools with spirit: Nurturing the inner lives of children and teachers* (pp. 39-52). Boston: Beacon Press.

Bronfenbrenner, U. (1986). Ecology of the family as a context for human development: Research perspectives. *Developmental Psychology, 22*(6), 723-742.

Bronfenbrenner, U. (1999). Environments in developmental perspective: Theoretical and operational models. In S. L. Friedman & T. D. Wachs (Eds.), *Measuring environment across the life span* (pp. 3-28). Washington, DC: American Psychological Association.

Chavkin, N. F., & Williams, R. (1993). *Families and schools in pluralistic society*. Albany, NY: State University of New York Press.

Coombs-Richardson, R., & Meisgeier, C. H. (2001). *Discipline options: Establishing a positive school climate*. Norwood, MA: Christopher-Gordon Publishers, Inc.

Coots, J. J., Bishop, K. D., Grenot-Scheyer, M., & Falvey, M. A. (1995). Practices in general education: Past and present. In M. A. Falvey (Ed.), *Inclusive and heterogeneous schooling: Assessment, curriculum, and instruction* (pp. 7-22). Baltimore: Paul H. Brookes.

Corson, D. (1998). Community-based education for indigenous cultures. Language, *Culture, and Curriculum, 11*(3), 238-249.

Cotton, K. (1995). *Effective schooling practices: A research synthesis (1995 update)*. Portland, OR: Northwest Regional Educational Laboratory.

Cross, W., Strauss, L., & Fhagen-Smith, P. (1999). African American identity development across the life span: Educational implications. In R. Sheets & E. Hollins (Eds.), *Racial and ethnic identity in school practices* (pp. 29-45). Mahwah, NJ: Lawrence Erlbaum Associates.

Dadson, S., & Horner, R. H. (1993). Manipulating setting events to decrease problem behaviors: A case study. *Teaching Exceptional Children, 25*(3), 53-58.

Dauber, S. L., & Epstein, J. L. (1993). Parents' attitudes and practices of involvement in inner-city elementary and middle schools. In N. F. Chavkin (Ed.), *Families and schools in a pluralistic society.* Albany, NY: State University of New York Press.

Delpit, L. (1991). A conversation with Lisa Delpit. *Language Arts, 71*, 554-545.

Delpit, L. (1995). *Other people's children: Cultural conflict in the classroom*. New York: The New Press.

Dennison, P. E., & Dennison, G. E. (1989). *Brain gym: Teacher's edition revised*. Ventura, CA: Edu-Kinesthetics, Inc.

Dunlap, G., Kern, L., dePerczel, M., Clarke, S., Wilson, D., Childs, K. E., White, R., Falk, G. (1993). Functional analysis of classroom variables for students with emotional and behavioral disorders. *Behavioral Disorders, 18*(4), 275-291.

Dunst, C. J., Trivette, C. M., & Deal, A. G. (1988). *Enabling and empowering families: Principles and guidelines for practice*. Cambridge, MA: Brookline Books.

Ellison, C. M., Boykin, A., Towns, D. P., & Stokes, A. (2000). *Classroom cultural ecology: The dynamics of classroom life in schools serving low-income African American children*. Washington, DC: Center for Research on the Education of Students at Risk.

Fawcett, S. B. (1991). Social validity: A note on methodology. *Journal of Applied Behavior Analysis, 24*(2), 235-239.

Flores, J. (1996). Authentic multiculturalism and nontraditional students: Voices from the "contact zone." *The Researcher, 11*(2), 20-35.

Fox, J. (1990). Ecology, environmental arrangement, and setting events: An interbehavioral perspective on organizing settings for behavioral development. *Education and Treatment of Children, 13*(4), 364-373.

Freedman, M. (1993). *The kindness of strangers*. San Francisco: Jossey-Bass.

Gable, R. A. (1996). A critical analysis of functional assessment: Issues for researchers and practitioners. *Behavioral Disorders, 22*(1), 36-40.

Gardner, H. (1983). *Frames of mind: The theory of multiples intelligences.* New York: Basic Books

Gardner, H. (1993). *Multiple intelligences: The theory in practice*. New York: Basic Books.

Gardner, W. I., Cole, C. L., Davidson, D. P., & Karan, O. C. (1986). Reducing aggression in individuals with developmental disabilities: An expanded stimulus control, assessment, and intervention model. *Education and Training of the Mentally Retarded, 21, 3-12.*

Gay, G. (1994). *A synthesis of scholarship in multicultural education*. Seattle, WA: North Central Regional Educational Laboratory.

Gay, G. (2000). *Culturally responsive teaching: Theory, research, and practice*. New York: Teachers College Press.

Geertz, C. (1973). *The interpretation of cultures*. New York: Basic Books.

Gollnick, D. M., & Chinn, P. C. (2002). *Multicultural education in a pluralistic society* (6th ed.). Upper Saddle River, NJ: Merrill/Prentice Hall.

Goodenough, W. (1987). Multi-culturalism as the normal human experience. In E. M. Eddy & W. L. Partridge (Eds.), *Applied anthropology in America* (2nd ed.). New York: Columbia University Press.

Grant, C. A., & Sleeter, C. E. (1998). *Turning on learning* (2nd ed.). Upper Saddle River, NJ: Merrill/Prentice Hall.

Gresham, F. M. (1989). Assessment of treatment integrity in school consultation and prereferral intervention. *School Psychology Review, 18*(1), 37-50.

Grimm, L. L. (1992). The Native American child in school: An ecological perspective. In M. I. Fine & C. Carlson (Eds.), *The handbook of family school intervention: A systems perspective* (pp. 102-118). Boston: Allyn & Bacon.

Guild, P. (1994). The culture/learning style connection. *Educational Leadership*, May, 16-21.

Hannaford, C. (1995). *Smart moves: Why learning is not all in your head.* Atlanta GA: Great Oceans Publishers.

Hanson, M. J. (1998). Ethnic, cultural, and language diversity in intervention settings. In E. Lynch & M. J. Hanson (Eds.), *Developing cross-cultural competence* (2nd ed.) (pp. 3-22). Baltimore: Paul H. Brookes.

Harding, C., London, L., & Safer, I. A. (2001). Teaching other people's ideas to other people's children: Integrating messages from education, psychology, and critical pedagogy. *Urban Education, 36*(4), 505-517.

Harding, J. W., Wacker, D. P., Berg, W. K., Cooper, L. J., Asmus, J., Mlela, K., & Muller, J. (1999). An analysis of choice making in the assessment of young children with severe behavior problems. *Journal of Applied Behavior Analysis, 32*(1), 63-82.

Harjo, S. S. (1999). The American Indian experiences. In. H. P. McAdoo (Ed.), *Family ethnicity: Strength in diversity.* Thousand Oaks, CA: Sage.

Harry, B. (1992). Reconstructing the participation of African American parents in special education. *Exceptional Children, 24*, 123-131.

Harry, B., Rueda, R., & Kalyanpur, M. (1999). Cultural reciprocity in sociocultural perspective: Adapting the normalization principle for family collaboration. *Exceptional Children, 66*(1), 123-136.

Heath, S. B., & McLaughlin, M. W. (Eds.). (1993). *Identity and inner-city youth: Beyond ethnicity and gender.* New York: Teachers College Press.

Heaviside, S., Rowand, C., Williams, C., Farris, E., Burns, S., & McArthur, E. (1998). *Violence and discipline problems in U.S. public schools: 1996-1997* (NCES 98-030). Washington, DC: U.S. Department of Education, National Center for Education Statistics.

Hodgkinson, C. (2001). Tomorrow, and tomorrow, and tomorrow: A post-postmodern purview. *International Journal of Leadership in Education, 4*(4), 297-307.

Horner, R. H. (1997). Encouraging a new applied science: A commentary on two papers addressing parent-professional partnerships in behavior support. *Journal of the Association for Persons with Severe Handicaps, 22*(4), 210-212.

Horner, R. H., Vaughn, B. J., Day, H. M., & Ard, W. R. (1996). The relationship between setting events and problem behavior. In S. K. Koegel, R. L. Koegel, & G. Dunlap (Eds.), *Positive behavior support: Including people with difficult behaviors in the community* (pp. 381-402). Baltimore: Paul H. Brookes.

In the best interests of all: A position paper of the Children's Behavioral Alliance. (2003). Children's Behavioral Alliance. Available: http://www.ccbd.net/printable/index.cfm?contentID=170 [2003, April 18].

Individuals with disabilities education act amendments of 1997 (1997). Available: http://www.ed.gov/offices/OSERS/IDEA/getregs.html [2001, June 6].

Inger, M. (1992). *Increasing the school involvement of Hispanic parents* (ERIC/CUE Digest No. 80). New York: ERIC Clearinghouse on Urban Education, Teachers College, Columbia University.

Jackson, R., & Harper, K. (2002). *Teacher planning and the universal design for learning.* Wakefield, MA: National Center on Accessing the General Curriculum.

Joe, J. R., & Malach, R. S. (1998). Families with Native American roots. In E. Lynch & M. J. Hanson (Eds.), *Developing cross-cultural competence* (pp. 127-164). Baltimore: Paul H. Brookes.

Johnson, D. W., & Johnson, R. T. (2002). Ensuring diversity is positive: Cooperative community, constructive conflict, and civic values. In J. S. Thousand, R. A. Villa, & A. I. Nevin (Eds.), *Creativity and collaborative learning: The practical guide to empowering students, teachers, and families* (2nd ed., pp. 197-208). Baltimore: Paul H. Brookes.

Jones, G. W., & Moomaw, S. (2002). *Lessons from Turtle Island: Native curriculum in early childhood classrooms.* St. Paul, MN: Redleaf Press.

Kagan, S. (1994). *Cooperative learning* (2nd ed.). San Juan Capistrano, CA: Kagan Cooperative Learning.

Kagan, S. (1998). New cooperative learning, multiple intelligences, and inclusion. In J. A. Putnam (Ed.), *Cooperative learning and strategies for inclusion* (pp. 105-136). Baltimore: Paul H. Brookes.

Kantor, J. R. (1970). An analysis of the experimental analysis of behavior (TEAB). *Journal of the Experimental Analysis of Behavior, 13*(1), 101-108.

Katz, M. (1997). Overcoming childhood adversities: Lessons learned from those who have "beat the odds." *Intervention in School and Clinic, 32*(4), 205-210.

Katz, S. R. (1999). Teaching in tensions: Latino immigrant youth, their teachers, and the structures of schooling. *Teachers College Record, 100*(4), 809-840.

Kennedy, C. H., & Itkonen, T. (1993). Effects of setting events on the problem behavior of students with severe disabilities. *Journal of Applied Behavior Analysis, 26*(3), 321-327.

Keogh, B. K., & Weisner, T. (1993). An ecocultural perspective on risk and protective factors in children's development: Implications for learning disabilities. *Learning Disabilities Research and Practice, 8*, 3-10.

Knoster, T., Kincaid, D., Brinkley, J., Malatchi, A., McFarland, J., Shannon, P., Hazelgrove, J., & Schall, C. (2000, October). Insights on implementing positive behavior support in schools. *TASH Newsletter, 26*, 23-25.

Ladson-Billings, G. (1994). *The dreamkeepers: Successful teachers of African American children.* San Francisco: Jossey-Bass.

Ladson-Billings, G. (2001). *Crossing over Canaan: The journey of new teachers in diverse classrooms.* San Francisco: Jossey-Bass.

LaFramboise, T. D., & Low, K. (1989). American Indian children and adolescents. In J. Gibbs & L. N. Huang (Eds.), *Children of color* (pp. 114-147). San Francisco, CA: Jossey-Bass.

Lesar, S., Trivette, C. M., & Dunst, C. J. (1995). Families of children and adolescents with special needs across the life span. *Exceptional Children, 62*(3), 197-199.

Lewis, M. C. (1993). *Beyond barriers: Involving Hispanic families in the education process.* Washington, DC: National Committee for Citizens in Education.

Lipson, M. Y., & Wixson, K. K. (1997). *Assessment and instruction of reading and writing disability.* New York: Longman.

Lynch, E. W. (1998). Developing cross-cultural competence. In E. Lynch & M. J. Hanson (Eds.), *Developing cross-cultural competence* (2nd ed.) (pp. 47-89). Baltimore: Paul H. Brookes.

Maag, J. W. (2001). Rewarded by punishment: Reflections on the disuse of positive reinforcement in schools. *Exceptional Children, 67*(2), 173-186.

Masten, A. S., Best, K. M., & Garmezy, N. (1990). Resilience and development: Contributions from the study of children who overcome adversity. *Development and Psychopathology, 2*, 425-444.

Masten, A. S., Morison, P., Pellegrini, D., & Tellegen, A. (1990). Competence under stress: Risk and protective factors. In J. Rolf, A. S. Masten, D. Cicchetti, Neuchterlein, & S. Weintraub (Eds.), *Risk and protective factors in the development of psychopathology* (pp. 236-256). New York: Cambridge University Press.

Mastropieri, M. A., & Scruggs, T. E. (2000). *The inclusive classroom: Strategies for effective instruction.* Upper Saddle River, NJ: Merrill/Prentice Hall.

Mayer, G. R. (1995). Preventing antisocial behavior in the schools. *Journal of Applied Behavior Analysis, 28*(4), 467-478.

McGill, P. (1999). Establishing operations: Implications for the assessment, treatment, and prevention of problem behavior. *Journal of Applied Behavior Analysis, 32*(3), 393-418.

McLaughlin, B. (1996). *Educating all our students: Improving education for children from culturally and linguistically diverse backgrounds.* Santa Cruz, CA: University of California at Santa Cruz.

McLaughlin, B., & McLeod, B. (1996). *Educating all our students: Improving education for children from culturally and linguistically diverse backgrounds.* National Center for Research on Cultural Diversity and Second Language Learning. Available: http://www.ncela.gwu.edu/miscpubs/ncrcdsll/edall.htm [2003, May 27].

Meyer, G. R., Mitchell, L. K., Clementii, T., & Clement-Robertson, E. (1993). A dropout prevention program for at-risk high school students: Emphasizing consulting to promote positive climate. *Education and Treatment of Children, 16,* 135-146.

Michael, J. (2000). Implications and refinements of the establishing operation concept. *Journal of Applied Behavior Analysis, 33*(4), 401-410.

Miramontes, O. B., Nadeau, A., & Commins, N. L. (1997). *Restructuring schools for linguistic diversity.* New York: Teachers College Press.

Nicolau, S. & Ramos, C. L. (1990). *Together is better: Building strong relationships between schools and Hispanic parents.* Washington, DC: Hispanic Policy Development Project.

Nweke, W. (1994). *Racial differences in parental discipline practices.* ERIC Document Reproduction Services No. ED 388 741.

Paley, V. (1992). *You can't say you can't play.* Cambridge, MA: Harvard University Press.

Parette, H. P., & Petch-Hogan, B. (2001). Approaching families: Facilitating culturally/linguistically diverse family involvement. *Teaching Exceptional Children, 33*(2), 4-10.

Patterson, G. R. (1975). *Families: Applications of social learning to family life.* Champaign, IL: Research Press.

Peterson, K. D. (1986). Problem-finding in principals' work. *Peabody Journal of Education, 63*(1), 87-106.

Prater, M. A., Sileo, T. W., & Black, R. S. (2000). Preparing educators and related school personnel to work with at-risk students. *Teacher Education and Special Education, 23*(1), 51-64.

Pratt, M. L. (1998). Arts of the contact zone. In V. Zamel & R. Spack (Eds.), *Negotiating academic literacies: Teaching and learning across languages and cultures* (pp. 171-185). Mahwah, NJ: Lawrence Erlbaum Associates.

Putnam, J. W. (1998). The process of cooperative learning. In J. W. Putnam (Ed.), *Cooperative learning and strategies for inclusion* (2nd ed., pp. 17-47). Baltimore: Paul H. Brookes.

Raymer, A. L. (2001). *Pedagogy of place: Facilitation guide.* Lexington, KY: University of Kentucky Appalachian Center.

Resnick, L. B. (1987). Learning in school and out. Educational Researcher, 16(9), 13-20. *Responding to linguistic and cultural diversity: Recommendations for effective early childhood education. (1995). Washington, DC: National Association for the Education of Young Children*

Rethinking schools (2000). Bilingual education: A goal for all children. Author, *15*(2), accessed October, 11, 2003. Available: http://www.rethinkingschools.org/special_reports/bilingual/Himu151.shtml.

Rock, M. L. (2000). Parents as equal partners: Balancing the scales in IEP development. *Teaching Exceptional Children, 32*(6), 30-37.

Rumberger, R. W. (1995). Dropping out of middle school: A multilevel analysis of students and schools. *American Educational Research Journal, 32*(3), 583-625.

Sapon-Shevin, M. (1994). Cooperative learning and middle schools: What would it take to really do it right? *Theory Into Practice, 33*(3), 183-190.

Sapon-Shevin, M. (1998). Everyone here can play. *Educational Leadership, 56*(1).

Sapon-Shevin, M. (2001). Schools Fit for All. *Educational Leadership, 58*(4), 34-39.

Sapon-Shevin, M., Ayres, B. J., & Duncan, J. (2002). Cooperative learning and inclusion. In J. S. Thousand, R. A. Villa, & A. I. Nevin (Eds.), *Creativity and collaborative learning: The practical guide to empowering students, teachers, and families* (2nd ed., pp. 209-221). Baltimore: Paul H. Brookes.

Schmidt, R. J., Rozendal, M. S., & Greenman, G. G. (2002). Reading instruction in the inclusion classroom: Research-based practices. *Remedial and Special Education, 23*(3), 130-140.

Schwartz, W. (1994). *A guide to communicating with Asian American families.* New York: ERIC Clearinghouse on Urban Education, Teachers College, Columbia University.

Shores, R. E., Gunter, P. L., & Jack, S. L. (1993). Classroom management strategies: Are they setting events for coercion? *Behavior Disorders, 18*(2), 92-102.

Sinclair, M. F., Christenson, S. L., Evelo, D. L., & Hurley, C. M. (1998). Dropout prevention for youth with disabilities: Efficacy of a sustained school engagement procedure. *Exceptional Children, 65*(1), 7-21.

Skinner, D., Bailey, D. B., Jr., Correa, V., & Rodriguez, P. (1999). Narrating self and disability: Latino mother's construction of identities vis-a-vis their child with special needs. *Exceptional Children, 65*(4), 481-495.

Sleeter, C. (2000). Origins of multiculturalism. Rethinking Schools, 15 (1), accessed October 11, 2003. Available: http://www.rethinkingschools.org/special_reports/bilingual/Himu151.shtml.

Smith, S. (1989). Operating on a child's heart: A pedagogical view of hospitalization. *Phenomenology and Pedagogy, 7*, 145-162.

Spindler, G., & Spindler, L. (1994). *Pathways to cultural awareness: Cultural therapy with teachers and students.* Thousand Oaks, CA: Sage.

Spradley, G., & McCurdy, D. W. (Eds.) (2000). *Conformity and conflict: Readings in cultural anthropology* (10th ed.). Boston: Allyn & Bacon.

Sugai, G., & Horner, R. H. (1994). Including students with severe behavior problems in general education settings: Assumptions, challenges, and solutions. In J. Marr, G. Sugai, & G. Tindal (Eds.), *The Oregon Conference Monograph* (volume 6, pp. 109-120). Eugene, OR: University of Oregon.

Tatum, B. (1992). Talking about race, learning about racism: The application of racial identity development theory in the classroom. *Harvard Educational Review, 62*(1), 1-24.

Tomlinson, C. (1995). *How to differentiate instruction in mixed-ability classrooms.* Alexandria, VA: Association for Supervision and Curriculum Development.

Tomlinson, C. (2001). *How to differentiate instruction in mixed-ability classrooms* (2nd ed.). Alexandria, VA: Association for Supervision and Curriculum Development.

Tompkins, G. E. (2003). *Literacy for the 21st Century.* Upper Saddle River, NJ: Prentice Hall.

Turnbull, A. H., Edmonson, H., Griggs, P., Wickham, D., Sailor, W., Freeman, R., Guess, D., Lassen, S., McCart, A., Park, J., Riffel, L., Turnbull, R., & Warren, J. (2002). A blueprint for schoolwide positive behavior support: Implementation of three components. *Exceptional Children, 68*(3), 377-402

Turning points: Preparing American youth for the 21st century. (1998). New York: Carnegie Council on Adolescent Development.

Vaughn, B. J., Dunlap, G., Fox, L., Clarke, S., & Bucy, M. (1997). Parent-professional partnership in behavior support: A case study of community-based intervention. *Journal of the Association for Persons with Severe Handicaps, 22*(4), 186-197.

Wehlage, G. G., Rutter, R. A., Smith, G. A., Lesko, N., & Fernandez, R. R. (1989). *Reducing the risk: Schools as communities of support.* New York: Falmer.

Weigle, K. (1997). Positive behavior support as a model for promoting educational inclusion. *Journal of the Association for Persons with Severe Handicaps, 22*(1), 36-48.

Weiss, H. (2002). Evaluation's role in supporting initiative sustainability 2002. Retrieved October 10, 2003. Available: www.gse.harvard.edu/hfrp/pubs/onlinepubs/sustainability/index.html.

White-Clark, R., & Decker, L. E. (1996). *The "hard to reach" parent: Old challenges, new insights.* Boston: Mid Atlantic Center for Community Education.

Wilder, D. A., & Carr, J. E. (1998). Recent advances in the modification of establishing operations to reduce aberrant behavior. *Behavioral Interventions, 13*, 43-59.

Williams, B. T. (1997). *Collision or Connection? Using contact zones to consider the cross-cultural classroom.* Unpublished manuscript, University of New Hampshire.

Willis, W. (1998). Families with African American roots. In E. Lynch & M. J. Hanson, (Eds.), *Developing cross-cultural competence* (2nd ed., pp. 165-207). Baltimore: Paul H. Brookes.

Wolfensberger, W. (1972). *The principle of normalization in human services.* Toronto: National Institute on Mental Retardation.

Yukl, G. (1994). *Managerial leadership and the effective principal.* New York: National Conference on the Principalship, National Institute of Education.

Xu, J. (2002). *Middle school family involvement in urban settings: Perspectives from minority students and their families.* Paper presented at the annual meeting of the American Educational Research Association, Seattle. Cambridge, MA: Harvard Family Research Institute.